C-2741   CAREER EXAMINATION SERIES

This is your
PASSBOOK for...

Drug & Alcohol Counselor

Test Preparation Study Guide
Questions & Answers

NATIONAL LEARNING CORPORATION®

COPYRIGHT NOTICE

This book is SOLELY intended for, is sold ONLY to, and its use is RESTRICTED to individual, bona fide applicants or candidates who qualify by virtue of having seriously filed applications for appropriate license, certificate, professional and/or promotional advancement, higher school matriculation, scholarship, or other legitimate requirements of education and/or governmental authorities.

This book is NOT intended for use, class instruction, tutoring, training, duplication, copying, reprinting, excerption, or adaptation, etc., by:

1) Other publishers
2) Proprietors and/or Instructors of "Coaching" and/or Preparatory Courses
3) Personnel and/or Training Divisions of commercial, industrial, and governmental organizations
4) Schools, colleges, or universities and/or their departments and staffs, including teachers and other personnel
5) Testing Agencies or Bureaus
6) Study groups which seek by the purchase of a single volume to copy and/or duplicate and/or adapt this material for use by the group as a whole without having purchased individual volumes for each of the members of the group
7) Et al.

Such persons would be in violation of appropriate Federal and State statutes.

PROVISION OF LICENSING AGREEMENTS – Recognized educational, commercial, industrial, and governmental institutions and organizations, and others legitimately engaged in educational pursuits, including training, testing, and measurement activities, may address request for a licensing agreement to the copyright owners, who will determine whether, and under what conditions, including fees and charges, the materials in this book may be used them. In other words, a licensing facility exists for the legitimate use of the material in this book on other than an individual basis. However, it is asseverated and affirmed here that the material in this book CANNOT be used without the receipt of the express permission of such a licensing agreement from the Publishers. Inquiries re licensing should be addressed to the company, attention rights and permissions department.

All rights reserved, including the right of reproduction in whole or in part, in any form or by any means, electronic or mechanical, including photocopying, recording, or by any information storage and retrieval system, without permission in writing from the Publisher.

Copyright © 2024 by
National Learning Corporation

212 Michael Drive, Syosset, NY 11791
(516) 921-8888 • www.passbooks.com
E-mail: info@passbooks.com

PUBLISHED IN THE UNITED STATES OF AMERICA

PASSBOOK® SERIES

THE *PASSBOOK® SERIES* has been created to prepare applicants and candidates for the ultimate academic battlefield – the examination room.

At some time in our lives, each and every one of us may be required to take an examination – for validation, matriculation, admission, qualification, registration, certification, or licensure.

Based on the assumption that every applicant or candidate has met the basic formal educational standards, has taken the required number of courses, and read the necessary texts, the *PASSBOOK® SERIES* furnishes the one special preparation which may assure passing with confidence, instead of failing with insecurity. Examination questions – together with answers – are furnished as the basic vehicle for study so that the mysteries of the examination and its compounding difficulties may be eliminated or diminished by a sure method.

This book is meant to help you pass your examination provided that you qualify and are serious in your objective.

The entire field is reviewed through the huge store of content information which is succinctly presented through a provocative and challenging approach – the question-and-answer method.

A climate of success is established by furnishing the correct answers at the end of each test.

You soon learn to recognize types of questions, forms of questions, and patterns of questioning. You may even begin to anticipate expected outcomes.

You perceive that many questions are repeated or adapted so that you can gain acute insights, which may enable you to score many sure points.

You learn how to confront new questions, or types of questions, and to attack them confidently and work out the correct answers.

You note objectives and emphases, and recognize pitfalls and dangers, so that you may make positive educational adjustments.

Moreover, you are kept fully informed in relation to new concepts, methods, practices, and directions in the field.

You discover that you are actually taking the examination all the time: you are preparing for the examination by "taking" an examination, not by reading extraneous and/or supererogatory textbooks.

In short, this PASSBOOK®, used directedly, should be an important factor in helping you to pass your test.

DRUG AND ALCOHOL COUNSELOR

DUTIES
An employee in this class provides professional screening and counseling services in the implementation of a drug and alcohol abuse prevention and/or treatment program. Work includes interviewing, monitoring and counseling clients, as well as advising and assisting clients with other substance abuse related problems. Develops and conducts seminars, workshops and training programs on the subject of drug and alcohol abuse. Performs related duties as required.

SCOPE OF THE EXAMINATION
The written test will cover knowledge and abilities in such areas as:

1. Alcohol, alcoholism and related problems;
2. Drugs, drug abuse and related problems;
3. Principles and practices of counseling;
4. Community organization, resources and relations; and
5. Preparing written material.

HOW TO TAKE A TEST

I. YOU MUST PASS AN EXAMINATION

A. WHAT EVERY CANDIDATE SHOULD KNOW

Examination applicants often ask us for help in preparing for the written test. What can I study in advance? What kinds of questions will be asked? How will the test be given? How will the papers be graded?

As an applicant for a civil service examination, you may be wondering about some of these things. Our purpose here is to suggest effective methods of advance study and to describe civil service examinations.

Your chances for success on this examination can be increased if you know how to prepare. Those "pre-examination jitters" can be reduced if you know what to expect. You can even experience an adventure in good citizenship if you know why civil service exams are given.

B. WHY ARE CIVIL SERVICE EXAMINATIONS GIVEN?

Civil service examinations are important to you in two ways. As a citizen, you want public jobs filled by employees who know how to do their work. As a job seeker, you want a fair chance to compete for that job on an equal footing with other candidates. The best-known means of accomplishing this two-fold goal is the competitive examination.

Exams are widely publicized throughout the nation. They may be administered for jobs in federal, state, city, municipal, town or village governments or agencies.

Any citizen may apply, with some limitations, such as the age or residence of applicants. Your experience and education may be reviewed to see whether you meet the requirements for the particular examination. When these requirements exist, they are reasonable and applied consistently to all applicants. Thus, a competitive examination may cause you some uneasiness now, but it is your privilege and safeguard.

C. HOW ARE CIVIL SERVICE EXAMS DEVELOPED?

Examinations are carefully written by trained technicians who are specialists in the field known as "psychological measurement," in consultation with recognized authorities in the field of work that the test will cover. These experts recommend the subject matter areas or skills to be tested; only those knowledges or skills important to your success on the job are included. The most reliable books and source materials available are used as references. Together, the experts and technicians judge the difficulty level of the questions.

Test technicians know how to phrase questions so that the problem is clearly stated. Their ethics do not permit "trick" or "catch" questions. Questions may have been tried out on sample groups, or subjected to statistical analysis, to determine their usefulness.

Written tests are often used in combination with performance tests, ratings of training and experience, and oral interviews. All of these measures combine to form the best-known means of finding the right person for the right job.

II. HOW TO PASS THE WRITTEN TEST

A. NATURE OF THE EXAMINATION

To prepare intelligently for civil service examinations, you should know how they differ from school examinations you have taken. In school you were assigned certain definite pages to read or subjects to cover. The examination questions were quite detailed and usually emphasized memory. Civil service exams, on the other hand, try to discover your present ability to perform the duties of a position, plus your potentiality to learn these duties. In other words, a civil service exam attempts to predict how successful you will be. Questions cover such a broad area that they cannot be as minute and detailed as school exam questions.

In the public service similar kinds of work, or positions, are grouped together in one "class." This process is known as *position-classification*. All the positions in a class are paid according to the salary range for that class. One class title covers all of these positions, and they are all tested by the same examination.

B. FOUR BASIC STEPS

1) Study the announcement

How, then, can you know what subjects to study? Our best answer is: "Learn as much as possible about the class of positions for which you've applied." The exam will test the knowledge, skills and abilities needed to do the work.

Your most valuable source of information about the position you want is the official exam announcement. This announcement lists the training and experience qualifications. Check these standards and apply only if you come reasonably close to meeting them.

The brief description of the position in the examination announcement offers some clues to the subjects which will be tested. Think about the job itself. Review the duties in your mind. Can you perform them, or are there some in which you are rusty? Fill in the blank spots in your preparation.

Many jurisdictions preview the written test in the exam announcement by including a section called "Knowledge and Abilities Required," "Scope of the Examination," or some similar heading. Here you will find out specifically what fields will be tested.

2) Review your own background

Once you learn in general what the position is all about, and what you need to know to do the work, ask yourself which subjects you already know fairly well and which need improvement. You may wonder whether to concentrate on improving your strong areas or on building some background in your fields of weakness. When the announcement has specified "some knowledge" or "considerable knowledge," or has used adjectives like "beginning principles of…" or "advanced … methods," you can get a clue as to the number and difficulty of questions to be asked in any given field. More questions, and hence broader coverage, would be included for those subjects which are more important in the work. Now weigh your strengths and weaknesses against the job requirements and prepare accordingly.

3) Determine the level of the position

Another way to tell how intensively you should prepare is to understand the level of the job for which you are applying. Is it the entering level? In other words, is this the position in which beginners in a field of work are hired? Or is it an intermediate or advanced level? Sometimes this is indicated by such words as "Junior" or "Senior" in the class title. Other jurisdictions use Roman numerals to designate the level – Clerk I, Clerk II, for example. The word "Supervisor" sometimes appears in the title. If the level is not indicated by the title, check the description of duties. Will you be working under very close supervision, or will you have responsibility for independent decisions in this work?

4) Choose appropriate study materials

Now that you know the subjects to be examined and the relative amount of each subject to be covered, you can choose suitable study materials. For beginning level jobs, or even advanced ones, if you have a pronounced weakness in some aspect of your training, read a modern, standard textbook in that field. Be sure it is up to date and has general coverage. Such books are normally available at your library, and the librarian will be glad to help you locate one. For entry-level positions, questions of appropriate difficulty are chosen -- neither highly advanced questions, nor those too simple. Such questions require careful thought but not advanced training.

If the position for which you are applying is technical or advanced, you will read more advanced, specialized material. If you are already familiar with the basic principles of your field, elementary textbooks would waste your time. Concentrate on advanced textbooks and technical periodicals. Think through the concepts and review difficult problems in your field.

These are all general sources. You can get more ideas on your own initiative, following these leads. For example, training manuals and publications of the government agency which employs workers in your field can be useful, particularly for technical and professional positions. A letter or visit to the government department involved may result in more specific study suggestions, and certainly will provide you with a more definite idea of the exact nature of the position you are seeking.

III. KINDS OF TESTS

Tests are used for purposes other than measuring knowledge and ability to perform specified duties. For some positions, it is equally important to test ability to make adjustments to new situations or to profit from training. In others, basic mental abilities not dependent on information are essential. Questions which test these things may not appear as pertinent to the duties of the position as those which test for knowledge and information. Yet they are often highly important parts of a fair examination. For very general questions, it is almost impossible to help you direct your study efforts. What we can do is to point out some of the more common of these general abilities needed in public service positions and describe some typical questions.

1) General information

Broad, general information has been found useful for predicting job success in some kinds of work. This is tested in a variety of ways, from vocabulary lists to questions about current events. Basic background in some field of work, such as sociology or economics, may be sampled in a group of questions. Often these are principles which have become familiar to most persons through exposure rather than through formal training. It is difficult to advise you how to study for these questions; being alert to the world around you is our best suggestion.

2) Verbal ability

An example of an ability needed in many positions is verbal or language ability. Verbal ability is, in brief, the ability to use and understand words. Vocabulary and grammar tests are typical measures of this ability. Reading comprehension or paragraph interpretation questions are common in many kinds of civil service tests. You are given a paragraph of written material and asked to find its central meaning.

3) Numerical ability

Number skills can be tested by the familiar arithmetic problem, by checking paired lists of numbers to see which are alike and which are different, or by interpreting charts and graphs. In the latter test, a graph may be printed in the test booklet which you are asked to use as the basis for answering questions.

4) Observation

A popular test for law-enforcement positions is the observation test. A picture is shown to you for several minutes, then taken away. Questions about the picture test your ability to observe both details and larger elements.

5) Following directions

In many positions in the public service, the employee must be able to carry out written instructions dependably and accurately. You may be given a chart with several columns, each column listing a variety of information. The questions require you to carry out directions involving the information given in the chart.

6) Skills and aptitudes

Performance tests effectively measure some manual skills and aptitudes. When the skill is one in which you are trained, such as typing or shorthand, you can practice. These tests are often very much like those given in business school or high school courses. For many of the other skills and aptitudes, however, no short-time preparation can be made. Skills and abilities natural to you or that you have developed throughout your lifetime are being tested.

Many of the general questions just described provide all the data needed to answer the questions and ask you to use your reasoning ability to find the answers. Your best preparation for these tests, as well as for tests of facts and ideas, is to be at your physical and mental best. You, no doubt, have your own methods of getting into an exam-taking mood and keeping "in shape." The next section lists some ideas on this subject.

IV. KINDS OF QUESTIONS

Only rarely is the "essay" question, which you answer in narrative form, used in civil service tests. Civil service tests are usually of the short-answer type. Full instructions for answering these questions will be given to you at the examination. But in case this is your first experience with short-answer questions and separate answer sheets, here is what you need to know:

1) Multiple-choice Questions

Most popular of the short-answer questions is the "multiple choice" or "best answer" question. It can be used, for example, to test for factual knowledge, ability to solve problems or judgment in meeting situations found at work.

A multiple-choice question is normally one of three types—
- It can begin with an incomplete statement followed by several possible endings. You are to find the one ending which *best* completes the statement, although some of the others may not be entirely wrong.
- It can also be a complete statement in the form of a question which is answered by choosing one of the statements listed.

- It can be in the form of a problem – again you select the best answer.

Here is an example of a multiple-choice question with a discussion which should give you some clues as to the method for choosing the right answer:

When an employee has a complaint about his assignment, the action which will *best* help him overcome his difficulty is to
    A. discuss his difficulty with his coworkers
    B. take the problem to the head of the organization
    C. take the problem to the person who gave him the assignment
    D. say nothing to anyone about his complaint

In answering this question, you should study each of the choices to find which is best. Consider choice "A" – Certainly an employee may discuss his complaint with fellow employees, but no change or improvement can result, and the complaint remains unresolved. Choice "B" is a poor choice since the head of the organization probably does not know what assignment you have been given, and taking your problem to him is known as "going over the head" of the supervisor. The supervisor, or person who made the assignment, is the person who can clarify it or correct any injustice. Choice "C" is, therefore, correct. To say nothing, as in choice "D," is unwise. Supervisors have and interest in knowing the problems employees are facing, and the employee is seeking a solution to his problem.

2) True/False Questions

The "true/false" or "right/wrong" form of question is sometimes used. Here a complete statement is given. Your job is to decide whether the statement is right or wrong.

SAMPLE: A roaming cell-phone call to a nearby city costs less than a non-roaming call to a distant city.

This statement is wrong, or false, since roaming calls are more expensive.

This is not a complete list of all possible question forms, although most of the others are variations of these common types. You will always get complete directions for answering questions. Be sure you understand *how* to mark your answers – ask questions until you do.

V. RECORDING YOUR ANSWERS

Computer terminals are used more and more today for many different kinds of exams.

For an examination with very few applicants, you may be told to record your answers in the test booklet itself. Separate answer sheets are much more common. If this separate answer sheet is to be scored by machine – and this is often the case – it is highly important that you mark your answers correctly in order to get credit.

An electronic scoring machine is often used in civil service offices because of the speed with which papers can be scored. Machine-scored answer sheets must be marked with a pencil, which will be given to you. This pencil has a high graphite content which responds to the electronic scoring machine. As a matter of fact, stray dots may register as answers, so do not let your pencil rest on the answer sheet while you are pondering the correct answer. Also, if your pencil lead breaks or is otherwise defective, ask for another.

Since the answer sheet will be dropped in a slot in the scoring machine, be careful not to bend the corners or get the paper crumpled.

The answer sheet normally has five vertical columns of numbers, with 30 numbers to a column. These numbers correspond to the question numbers in your test booklet. After each number, going across the page are four or five pairs of dotted lines. These short dotted lines have small letters or numbers above them. The first two pairs may also have a "T" or "F" above the letters. This indicates that the first two pairs only are to be used if the questions are of the true-false type. If the questions are multiple choice, disregard the "T" and "F" and pay attention only to the small letters or numbers.

Answer your questions in the manner of the sample that follows:

32. The largest city in the United States is
    A. Washington, D.C.
    B. New York City
    C. Chicago
    D. Detroit
    E. San Francisco

1) Choose the answer you think is best. (New York City is the largest, so "B" is correct.)
2) Find the row of dotted lines numbered the same as the question you are answering. (Find row number 32)
3) Find the pair of dotted lines corresponding to the answer. (Find the pair of lines under the mark "B.")
4) Make a solid black mark between the dotted lines.

VI. BEFORE THE TEST

Common sense will help you find procedures to follow to get ready for an examination. Too many of us, however, overlook these sensible measures. Indeed, nervousness and fatigue have been found to be the most serious reasons why applicants fail to do their best on civil service tests. Here is a list of reminders:

- Begin your preparation early – Don't wait until the last minute to go scurrying around for books and materials or to find out what the position is all about.
- Prepare continuously – An hour a night for a week is better than an all-night cram session. This has been definitely established. What is more, a night a week for a month will return better dividends than crowding your study into a shorter period of time.
- Locate the place of the exam – You have been sent a notice telling you when and where to report for the examination. If the location is in a different town or otherwise unfamiliar to you, it would be well to inquire the best route and learn something about the building.
- Relax the night before the test – Allow your mind to rest. Do not study at all that night. Plan some mild recreation or diversion; then go to bed early and get a good night's sleep.
- Get up early enough to make a leisurely trip to the place for the test – This way unforeseen events, traffic snarls, unfamiliar buildings, etc. will not upset you.
- Dress comfortably – A written test is not a fashion show. You will be known by number and not by name, so wear something comfortable.

- Leave excess paraphernalia at home – Shopping bags and odd bundles will get in your way. You need bring only the items mentioned in the official notice you received; usually everything you need is provided. Do not bring reference books to the exam. They will only confuse those last minutes and be taken away from you when in the test room.
- Arrive somewhat ahead of time – If because of transportation schedules you must get there very early, bring a newspaper or magazine to take your mind off yourself while waiting.
- Locate the examination room – When you have found the proper room, you will be directed to the seat or part of the room where you will sit. Sometimes you are given a sheet of instructions to read while you are waiting. Do not fill out any forms until you are told to do so; just read them and be prepared.
- Relax and prepare to listen to the instructions
- If you have any physical problem that may keep you from doing your best, be sure to tell the test administrator. If you are sick or in poor health, you really cannot do your best on the exam. You can come back and take the test some other time.

VII. AT THE TEST

The day of the test is here and you have the test booklet in your hand. The temptation to get going is very strong. Caution! There is more to success than knowing the right answers. You must know how to identify your papers and understand variations in the type of short-answer question used in this particular examination. Follow these suggestions for maximum results from your efforts:

1) Cooperate with the monitor

The test administrator has a duty to create a situation in which you can be as much at ease as possible. He will give instructions, tell you when to begin, check to see that you are marking your answer sheet correctly, and so on. He is not there to guard you, although he will see that your competitors do not take unfair advantage. He wants to help you do your best.

2) Listen to all instructions

Don't jump the gun! Wait until you understand all directions. In most civil service tests you get more time than you need to answer the questions. So don't be in a hurry. Read each word of instructions until you clearly understand the meaning. Study the examples, listen to all announcements and follow directions. Ask questions if you do not understand what to do.

3) Identify your papers

Civil service exams are usually identified by number only. You will be assigned a number; you must not put your name on your test papers. Be sure to copy your number correctly. Since more than one exam may be given, copy your exact examination title.

4) Plan your time

Unless you are told that a test is a "speed" or "rate of work" test, speed itself is usually not important. Time enough to answer all the questions will be provided, but this does not mean that you have all day. An overall time limit has been set. Divide the total time (in minutes) by the number of questions to determine the approximate time you have for each question.

5) Do not linger over difficult questions

If you come across a difficult question, mark it with a paper clip (useful to have along) and come back to it when you have been through the booklet. One caution if you do this – be sure to skip a number on your answer sheet as well. Check often to be sure that you have not lost your place and that you are marking in the row numbered the same as the question you are answering.

6) Read the questions

Be sure you know what the question asks! Many capable people are unsuccessful because they failed to *read* the questions correctly.

7) Answer all questions

Unless you have been instructed that a penalty will be deducted for incorrect answers, it is better to guess than to omit a question.

8) Speed tests

It is often better NOT to guess on speed tests. It has been found that on timed tests people are tempted to spend the last few seconds before time is called in marking answers at random – without even reading them – in the hope of picking up a few extra points. To discourage this practice, the instructions may warn you that your score will be "corrected" for guessing. That is, a penalty will be applied. The incorrect answers will be deducted from the correct ones, or some other penalty formula will be used.

9) Review your answers

If you finish before time is called, go back to the questions you guessed or omitted to give them further thought. Review other answers if you have time.

10) Return your test materials

If you are ready to leave before others have finished or time is called, take ALL your materials to the monitor and leave quietly. Never take any test material with you. The monitor can discover whose papers are not complete, and taking a test booklet may be grounds for disqualification.

VIII. EXAMINATION TECHNIQUES

1) Read the general instructions carefully. These are usually printed on the first page of the exam booklet. As a rule, these instructions refer to the timing of the examination; the fact that you should not start work until the signal and must stop work at a signal, etc. If there are any *special* instructions, such as a choice of questions to be answered, make sure that you note this instruction carefully.

2) When you are ready to start work on the examination, that is as soon as the signal has been given, read the instructions to each question booklet, underline any key words or phrases, such as *least, best, outline, describe* and the like. In this way you will tend to answer as requested rather than discover on reviewing your paper that you *listed without describing*, that you selected the *worst* choice rather than the *best* choice, etc.

3) If the examination is of the objective or multiple-choice type – that is, each question will also give a series of possible answers: A, B, C or D, and you are called upon to select the best answer and write the letter next to that answer on your answer paper – it is advisable to start answering each question in turn. There may be anywhere from 50 to 100 such questions in the three or four hours allotted and you can see how much time would be taken if you read through all the questions before beginning to answer any. Furthermore, if you come across a question or group of questions which you know would be difficult to answer, it would undoubtedly affect your handling of all the other questions.

4) If the examination is of the essay type and contains but a few questions, it is a moot point as to whether you should read all the questions before starting to answer any one. Of course, if you are given a choice – say five out of seven and the like – then it is essential to read all the questions so you can eliminate the two that are most difficult. If, however, you are asked to answer all the questions, there may be danger in trying to answer the easiest one first because you may find that you will spend too much time on it. The best technique is to answer the first question, then proceed to the second, etc.

5) Time your answers. Before the exam begins, write down the time it started, then add the time allowed for the examination and write down the time it must be completed, then divide the time available somewhat as follows:
   - If 3-1/2 hours are allowed, that would be 210 minutes. If you have 80 objective-type questions, that would be an average of 2-1/2 minutes per question. Allow yourself no more than 2 minutes per question, or a total of 160 minutes, which will permit about 50 minutes to review.
   - If for the time allotment of 210 minutes there are 7 essay questions to answer, that would average about 30 minutes a question. Give yourself only 25 minutes per question so that you have about 35 minutes to review.

6) The most important instruction is to *read each question* and make sure you know what is wanted. The second most important instruction is to *time yourself properly* so that you answer every question. The third most important instruction is to *answer every question*. Guess if you have to but include something for each question. Remember that you will receive no credit for a blank and will probably receive some credit if you write something in answer to an essay question. If you guess a letter – say "B" for a multiple-choice question – you may have guessed right. If you leave a blank as an answer to a multiple-choice question, the examiners may respect your feelings but it will not add a point to your score. Some exams may penalize you for wrong answers, so in such cases *only*, you may not want to guess unless you have some basis for your answer.

7) Suggestions
   a. Objective-type questions
      1. Examine the question booklet for proper sequence of pages and questions
      2. Read all instructions carefully
      3. Skip any question which seems too difficult; return to it after all other questions have been answered
      4. Apportion your time properly; do not spend too much time on any single question or group of questions

5. Note and underline key words – *all, most, fewest, least, best, worst, same, opposite,* etc.
6. Pay particular attention to negatives
7. Note unusual option, e.g., unduly long, short, complex, different or similar in content to the body of the question
8. Observe the use of "hedging" words – *probably, may, most likely,* etc.
9. Make sure that your answer is put next to the same number as the question
10. Do not second-guess unless you have good reason to believe the second answer is definitely more correct
11. Cross out original answer if you decide another answer is more accurate; do not erase until you are ready to hand your paper in
12. Answer all questions; guess unless instructed otherwise
13. Leave time for review

b. Essay questions
1. Read each question carefully
2. Determine exactly what is wanted. Underline key words or phrases.
3. Decide on outline or paragraph answer
4. Include many different points and elements unless asked to develop any one or two points or elements
5. Show impartiality by giving pros and cons unless directed to select one side only
6. Make and write down any assumptions you find necessary to answer the questions
7. Watch your English, grammar, punctuation and choice of words
8. Time your answers; don't crowd material

8) Answering the essay question

Most essay questions can be answered by framing the specific response around several key words or ideas. Here are a few such key words or ideas:

M's: manpower, materials, methods, money, management
P's: purpose, program, policy, plan, procedure, practice, problems, pitfalls, personnel, public relations

a. Six basic steps in handling problems:
1. Preliminary plan and background development
2. Collect information, data and facts
3. Analyze and interpret information, data and facts
4. Analyze and develop solutions as well as make recommendations
5. Prepare report and sell recommendations
6. Install recommendations and follow up effectiveness

b. Pitfalls to avoid
1. *Taking things for granted* – A statement of the situation does not necessarily imply that each of the elements is necessarily true; for example, a complaint may be invalid and biased so that all that can be taken for granted is that a complaint has been registered

2. *Considering only one side of a situation* – Wherever possible, indicate several alternatives and then point out the reasons you selected the best one
3. *Failing to indicate follow up* – Whenever your answer indicates action on your part, make certain that you will take proper follow-up action to see how successful your recommendations, procedures or actions turn out to be
4. *Taking too long in answering any single question* – Remember to time your answers properly

IX. AFTER THE TEST

Scoring procedures differ in detail among civil service jurisdictions although the general principles are the same. Whether the papers are hand-scored or graded by machine we have described, they are nearly always graded by number. That is, the person who marks the paper knows only the number – never the name – of the applicant. Not until all the papers have been graded will they be matched with names. If other tests, such as training and experience or oral interview ratings have been given, scores will be combined. Different parts of the examination usually have different weights. For example, the written test might count 60 percent of the final grade, and a rating of training and experience 40 percent. In many jurisdictions, veterans will have a certain number of points added to their grades.

After the final grade has been determined, the names are placed in grade order and an eligible list is established. There are various methods for resolving ties between those who get the same final grade – probably the most common is to place first the name of the person whose application was received first. Job offers are made from the eligible list in the order the names appear on it. You will be notified of your grade and your rank as soon as all these computations have been made. This will be done as rapidly as possible.

People who are found to meet the requirements in the announcement are called "eligibles." Their names are put on a list of eligible candidates. An eligible's chances of getting a job depend on how high he stands on this list and how fast agencies are filling jobs from the list.

When a job is to be filled from a list of eligibles, the agency asks for the names of people on the list of eligibles for that job. When the civil service commission receives this request, it sends to the agency the names of the three people highest on this list. Or, if the job to be filled has specialized requirements, the office sends the agency the names of the top three persons who meet these requirements from the general list.

The appointing officer makes a choice from among the three people whose names were sent to him. If the selected person accepts the appointment, the names of the others are put back on the list to be considered for future openings.

That is the rule in hiring from all kinds of eligible lists, whether they are for typist, carpenter, chemist, or something else. For every vacancy, the appointing officer has his choice of any one of the top three eligibles on the list. This explains why the person whose name is on top of the list sometimes does not get an appointment when some of the persons lower on the list do. If the appointing officer chooses the second or third eligible, the No. 1 eligible does not get a job at once, but stays on the list until he is appointed or the list is terminated.

X. HOW TO PASS THE INTERVIEW TEST

The examination for which you applied requires an oral interview test. You have already taken the written test and you are now being called for the interview test – the final part of the formal examination.

You may think that it is not possible to prepare for an interview test and that there are no procedures to follow during an interview. Our purpose is to point out some things you can do in advance that will help you and some good rules to follow and pitfalls to avoid while you are being interviewed.

What is an interview supposed to test?

The written examination is designed to test the technical knowledge and competence of the candidate; the oral is designed to evaluate intangible qualities, not readily measured otherwise, and to establish a list showing the relative fitness of each candidate – as measured against his competitors – for the position sought. Scoring is not on the basis of "right" and "wrong," but on a sliding scale of values ranging from "not passable" to "outstanding." As a matter of fact, it is possible to achieve a relatively low score without a single "incorrect" answer because of evident weakness in the qualities being measured.

Occasionally, an examination may consist entirely of an oral test – either an individual or a group oral. In such cases, information is sought concerning the technical knowledges and abilities of the candidate, since there has been no written examination for this purpose. More commonly, however, an oral test is used to supplement a written examination.

Who conducts interviews?

The composition of oral boards varies among different jurisdictions. In nearly all, a representative of the personnel department serves as chairman. One of the members of the board may be a representative of the department in which the candidate would work. In some cases, "outside experts" are used, and, frequently, a businessman or some other representative of the general public is asked to serve. Labor and management or other special groups may be represented. The aim is to secure the services of experts in the appropriate field.

However the board is composed, it is a good idea (and not at all improper or unethical) to ascertain in advance of the interview who the members are and what groups they represent. When you are introduced to them, you will have some idea of their backgrounds and interests, and at least you will not stutter and stammer over their names.

What should be done before the interview?

While knowledge about the board members is useful and takes some of the surprise element out of the interview, there is other preparation which is more substantive. It *is* possible to prepare for an oral interview – in several ways:

1) Keep a copy of your application and review it carefully before the interview

This may be the only document before the oral board, and the starting point of the interview. Know what education and experience you have listed there, and the sequence and dates of all of it. Sometimes the board will ask you to review the highlights of your experience for them; you should not have to hem and haw doing it.

2) Study the class specification and the examination announcement

Usually, the oral board has one or both of these to guide them. The qualities, characteristics or knowledges required by the position sought are stated in these documents. They offer valuable clues as to the nature of the oral interview. For example, if the job involves supervisory responsibilities, the announcement will usually indicate that knowledge of modern supervisory methods and the qualifications of the candidate as a supervisor will be tested. If so, you can expect such questions, frequently in the form of a hypothetical situation which you are expected to solve. NEVER go into an oral without knowledge of the duties and responsibilities of the job you seek.

3) Think through each qualification required

Try to visualize the kind of questions you would ask if you were a board member. How well could you answer them? Try especially to appraise your own knowledge and background in each area, *measured against the job sought*, and identify any areas in which you are weak. Be critical and realistic – do not flatter yourself.

4) Do some general reading in areas in which you feel you may be weak

For example, if the job involves supervision and your past experience has NOT, some general reading in supervisory methods and practices, particularly in the field of human relations, might be useful. Do NOT study agency procedures or detailed manuals. The oral board will be testing your understanding and capacity, not your memory.

5) Get a good night's sleep and watch your general health and mental attitude

You will want a clear head at the interview. Take care of a cold or any other minor ailment, and of course, no hangovers.

What should be done on the day of the interview?

Now comes the day of the interview itself. Give yourself plenty of time to get there. Plan to arrive somewhat ahead of the scheduled time, particularly if your appointment is in the fore part of the day. If a previous candidate fails to appear, the board might be ready for you a bit early. By early afternoon an oral board is almost invariably behind schedule if there are many candidates, and you may have to wait. Take along a book or magazine to read, or your application to review, but leave any extraneous material in the waiting room when you go in for your interview. In any event, relax and compose yourself.

The matter of dress is important. The board is forming impressions about you – from your experience, your manners, your attitude, and your appearance. Give your personal appearance careful attention. Dress your best, but not your flashiest. Choose conservative, appropriate clothing, and be sure it is immaculate. This is a business interview, and your appearance should indicate that you regard it as such. Besides, being well groomed and properly dressed will help boost your confidence.

Sooner or later, someone will call your name and escort you into the interview room. *This is it.* From here on you are on your own. It is too late for any more preparation. But remember, you asked for this opportunity to prove your fitness, and you are here because your request was granted.

What happens when you go in?

The usual sequence of events will be as follows: The clerk (who is often the board stenographer) will introduce you to the chairman of the oral board, who will introduce you to the other members of the board. Acknowledge the introductions before you sit down. Do not be surprised if you find a microphone facing you or a stenotypist sitting by. Oral interviews are usually recorded in the event of an appeal or other review.

Usually the chairman of the board will open the interview by reviewing the highlights of your education and work experience from your application – primarily for the benefit of the other members of the board, as well as to get the material into the record. Do not interrupt or comment unless there is an error or significant misinterpretation; if that is the case, do not hesitate. But do not quibble about insignificant matters. Also, he will usually ask you some question about your education, experience or your present job – partly to get you to start talking and to establish the interviewing "rapport." He may start the actual questioning, or turn it over to one of the other members. Frequently, each member undertakes the questioning on a particular area, one in which he is perhaps most competent, so you can expect each member to participate in the examination. Because time is limited, you may also expect some rather abrupt switches in the direction the questioning takes, so do not be upset by it. Normally, a board member will not pursue a single line of questioning unless he discovers a particular strength or weakness.

After each member has participated, the chairman will usually ask whether any member has any further questions, then will ask you if you have anything you wish to add. Unless you are expecting this question, it may floor you. Worse, it may start you off on an extended, extemporaneous speech. The board is not usually seeking more information. The question is principally to offer you a last opportunity to present further qualifications or to indicate that you have nothing to add. So, if you feel that a significant qualification or characteristic has been overlooked, it is proper to point it out in a sentence or so. Do not compliment the board on the thoroughness of their examination – they have been sketchy, and you know it. If you wish, merely say, "No thank you, I have nothing further to add." This is a point where you can "talk yourself out" of a good impression or fail to present an important bit of information. Remember, *you close the interview yourself.*

The chairman will then say, "That is all, Mr. _____, thank you." Do not be startled; the interview is over, and quicker than you think. Thank him, gather your belongings and take your leave. Save your sigh of relief for the other side of the door.

How to put your best foot forward

Throughout this entire process, you may feel that the board individually and collectively is trying to pierce your defenses, seek out your hidden weaknesses and embarrass and confuse you. Actually, this is not true. They are obliged to make an appraisal of your qualifications for the job you are seeking, and they want to see you in your best light. Remember, they must interview all candidates and a non-cooperative candidate may become a failure in spite of their best efforts to bring out his qualifications. Here are 15 suggestions that will help you:

1) Be natural – Keep your attitude confident, not cocky

If you are not confident that you can do the job, do not expect the board to be. Do not apologize for your weaknesses, try to bring out your strong points. The board is interested in a positive, not negative, presentation. Cockiness will antagonize any board member and make him wonder if you are covering up a weakness by a false show of strength.

2) Get comfortable, but don't lounge or sprawl

Sit erectly but not stiffly. A careless posture may lead the board to conclude that you are careless in other things, or at least that you are not impressed by the importance of the occasion. Either conclusion is natural, even if incorrect. Do not fuss with your clothing, a pencil or an ashtray. Your hands may occasionally be useful to emphasize a point; do not let them become a point of distraction.

3) Do not wisecrack or make small talk

This is a serious situation, and your attitude should show that you consider it as such. Further, the time of the board is limited – they do not want to waste it, and neither should you.

4) Do not exaggerate your experience or abilities

In the first place, from information in the application or other interviews and sources, the board may know more about you than you think. Secondly, you probably will not get away with it. An experienced board is rather adept at spotting such a situation, so do not take the chance.

5) If you know a board member, do not make a point of it, yet do not hide it

Certainly you are not fooling him, and probably not the other members of the board. Do not try to take advantage of your acquaintanceship – it will probably do you little good.

6) Do not dominate the interview

Let the board do that. They will give you the clues – do not assume that you have to do all the talking. Realize that the board has a number of questions to ask you, and do not try to take up all the interview time by showing off your extensive knowledge of the answer to the first one.

7) Be attentive

You only have 20 minutes or so, and you should keep your attention at its sharpest throughout. When a member is addressing a problem or question to you, give him your undivided attention. Address your reply principally to him, but do not exclude the other board members.

8) Do not interrupt

A board member may be stating a problem for you to analyze. He will ask you a question when the time comes. Let him state the problem, and wait for the question.

9) Make sure you understand the question

Do not try to answer until you are sure what the question is. If it is not clear, restate it in your own words or ask the board member to clarify it for you. However, do not haggle about minor elements.

10) Reply promptly but not hastily

A common entry on oral board rating sheets is "candidate responded readily," or "candidate hesitated in replies." Respond as promptly and quickly as you can, but do not jump to a hasty, ill-considered answer.

11) Do not be peremptory in your answers

A brief answer is proper – but do not fire your answer back. That is a losing game from your point of view. The board member can probably ask questions much faster than you can answer them.

12) Do not try to create the answer you think the board member wants

He is interested in what kind of mind you have and how it works – not in playing games. Furthermore, he can usually spot this practice and will actually grade you down on it.

13) Do not switch sides in your reply merely to agree with a board member

Frequently, a member will take a contrary position merely to draw you out and to see if you are willing and able to defend your point of view. Do not start a debate, yet do not surrender a good position. If a position is worth taking, it is worth defending.

14) Do not be afraid to admit an error in judgment if you are shown to be wrong

The board knows that you are forced to reply without any opportunity for careful consideration. Your answer may be demonstrably wrong. If so, admit it and get on with the interview.

15) Do not dwell at length on your present job

The opening question may relate to your present assignment. Answer the question but do not go into an extended discussion. You are being examined for a *new* job, not your present one. As a matter of fact, try to phrase ALL your answers in terms of the job for which you are being examined.

Basis of Rating

Probably you will forget most of these "do's" and "don'ts" when you walk into the oral interview room. Even remembering them all will not ensure you a passing grade. Perhaps you did not have the qualifications in the first place. But remembering them will help you to put your best foot forward, without treading on the toes of the board members.

Rumor and popular opinion to the contrary notwithstanding, an oral board wants you to make the best appearance possible. They know you are under pressure – but they also want to see how you respond to it as a guide to what your reaction would be under the pressures of the job you seek. They will be influenced by the degree of poise you display, the personal traits you show and the manner in which you respond.

ABOUT THIS BOOK

This book contains tests divided into Examination Sections. Go through each test, answering every question in the margin. We have also attached a sample answer sheet at the back of the book that can be removed and used. At the end of each test look at the answer key and check your answers. On the ones you got wrong, look at the right answer choice and learn. Do not fill in the answers first. Do not memorize the questions and answers, but understand the answer and principles involved. On your test, the questions will likely be different from the samples. Questions are changed and new ones added. If you understand these past questions you should have success with any changes that arise. Tests may consist of several types of questions. We have additional books on each subject should more study be advisable or necessary for you. Finally, the more you study, the better prepared you will be. This book is intended to be the last thing you study before you walk into the examination room. Prior study of relevant texts is also recommended. NLC publishes some of these in our Fundamental Series. Knowledge and good sense are important factors in passing your exam. Good luck also helps. So now study this Passbook, absorb the material contained within and take that knowledge into the examination. Then do your best to pass that exam.

EXAMINATION SECTION

EXAMINATION SECTION
TEST 1

DIRECTIONS: Each question or incomplete statement is followed by several suggested answers or completions. Select the one that BEST answers the question or completes the statement. *PRINT THE LETTER OF THE CORRECT ANSWER IN THE SPACE AT THE RIGHT.*

1. Methadone is a synthetic substitute for

    A. demerol
    B. morphine
    C. laudanum
    D. pentothal

    1.____

2. A family of synthetic drugs made from coal tar is the

    A. opiates
    B. cocaines
    C. bromides
    D. barbiturates

    2.____

3. A drug which does NOT cause physical addiction or withdrawal symptoms but is regulated by the government as a narcotic is

    A. codeine
    B. morphine
    C. cocaine
    D. heroin

    3.____

4. The term *tracks* is associated with the users of

    A. L.S.D.
    B. red devils
    C. methadone
    D. heroin

    4.____

5. Of the following drugs, the one that is a stimulant is

    A. alcohol
    B. amphetamines
    C. barbiturates
    D. opiates

    5.____

6. Amytal, Seconal and Nembutal are prescription drugs classified as

    A. barbiturates
    B. hallucinogens
    C. opiates
    D. amphetamines

    6.____

7. A drug which is classed legally as a narcotic while medically it is NOT is

    A. opium
    B. cocaine
    C. heroin
    D. codeine

    7.____

8. Of the following regarding barbiturates, the INCORRECT statement is:

    A. More people die as a result of acute intoxication from barbiturates than from any other drug poisoning
    B. Taking barbiturates along with alcoholic beverages may prove to be fatal
    C. The medicinal use of barbiturates has been prescribed for sedation, sleep-producing, epilepsy, and high blood pressure
    D. Barbiturates are not depressants

    8.____

9. The CORRECT association related to the special language of drug users is

    A. candy–hallucinogens
    B. cartwheels–tranquilizers
    C. bennies–barbiturates
    D. co-pilots–amphetamines

    9.____

10. As related to treatment and rehabilitation of drug abuse, the CORRECT association is

    A. detoxification—substituting a less harmful drug
    B. maintenance—peer group support
    C. encounter therapy—in-patient hospitalization
    D. therapeutic community—halfway house using former addicts

11. Methaqualone is used medically as a

    A. safe substitute for barbiturates
    B. non-addicting anti-convulsant
    C. prescription for sleeplessness
    D. prevention of skeletal abnormalities in human fetuses

12. All of the following statements concerning the intake of alcohol in the body are correct EXCEPT:

    A. Although alcohol has a caloric content, it is expended instead of being stored in the body.
    B. A small percentage of the alcohol taken into the body is eliminated through the lungs.
    C. Alcohol produces a feeling of warmth with an actual lowering of body temperature.
    D. Digestive changes are necessary before alcohol can be absorbed from the stomach.

13. All of the following characteristics predispose a person to alcoholism EXCEPT having

    A. little tolerance for frustration
    B. low energy levels and strong impulse control
    C. strong feelings of alienation
    D. conflicts in family relationships

14. The MOST effective approach for a teacher to use in an alcohol education unit is to

    A. stress the evils of alcoholism
    B. emphasize the importance of the freedom of the individual to make responsible choices
    C. present facts about alcohol to the students
    D. use the scare approach to discourage students from using alcohol

15. In developing a program of treatment of the alcoholic, the LEAST important consideration is

    A. hospitalization until completion of the treatment
    B. detoxification
    C. physical rehabilitation including nutritional assistance
    D. maintenance of abstinence

16. One of the EARLIEST effects of alcohol on the body is

    A. reduced heart action
    B. loss of equilibrium
    C. decrease in judgment and self-control
    D. blurred and double vision

17. It is CORRECT to state that the *immediate* effect of alcohol on the body is to 17.____

    A. constrict surface blood vessels
    B. decrease the rate of the heartbeat
    C. increase blood pressure
    D. decrease body temperature

18. Of the following concerning alcohol, the CORRECT statement is: 18.____

    A. Alcohol acts principally on the central nervous system
    B. As a rule, black coffee will do away with intoxication
    C. There are no individual differences among people which relate to alcoholism
    D. About 50% of the alcohol consumed is eliminated unchanged through the kidneys and lungs

19. As alcohol is oxidized in the body tissues, the energy it contains is 19.____

    A. used up in muscular activity
    B. used in accelerated activity of the nervous system
    C. stored in the body
    D. given off as heat

20. Of the following, the substance with addicting properties would be 20.____

    A. mescaline   B. phenobarbital
    C. librium   D. cocaine

21. When considered as a drug, the MOST accurate classification which describes alcohol is that it is a 21.____

    A. stimulant   B. depressant
    C. hallucinogen   D. tranquilizer

22. The MOST common signs and symptoms associated with the use of marijuana are 22.____

    A. thirst, drowsiness, and passiveness
    B. pink eyes, increased pulse rate, and hunger
    C. discomfort, anxiety. and general ataxia
    D. increased libido, decreased blood pressure, and pupil dilation

23. While under the influence of morphine, an addict will *usually* 23.____

    A. experience an abnormal dryness of the nose
    B. have contracted, pinpoint pupils of the eyes
    C. feel strong and superior and experience loss of fatigue
    D. be very talkative and will not listen to others

24. Of the following statements concerning drugs, the CORRECT one is: 24.____

    A. As a person's tolerance to barbiturates increases, his tolerance level to other drugs also increases.
    B. Many heroin addicts will use amphetamines when they cannot obtain heroin.
    C. Most experts consider barbiturate addiction more dangerous than heroin addiction.
    D. When skin popping, the user will most often inject directly into a vein.

25. The time between the consuming of alcohol and its beginning to be absorbed into the bloodstream may be *as little as* _____ minutes.   25.____

    A. 2   B. 5   C. 8   D. 10

26. All of the following statements concerning alcohol and its effect on the body are correct EXCEPT: 26.____

    A. The constant presence of alcohol impairs the liver cells in their ability to store glycogen
    B. At high concentrations, alcohol causes the lessening of gastric juice secretion
    C. Beriberi is one of the commonest deficiency diseases associated with alcoholism
    D. Alcohol increases the enzyme action in the stomach

27. The MOST severe withdrawal reactions result from addiction to   27.____

    A. cocaine   B. heroin
    C. barbiturates   D. mescaline

28. The difference between marijuana and heroin is that   28.____

    A. marijuana has no proven medical use
    B. heroin is more addictive
    C. pure heroin is better to use than pure marijuana
    D. the emotions are more directly affected by marijuana than by heroin

29. With regard to marijuana, the CORRECT statement is: 29.____

    A. More severe penalties will decrease the problem.
    B. Marijuana use usually leads to heroin use.
    C. Marijuana is harmless.
    D. Driving under the influence of marijuana is hazardous.

30. Of the following statements, it is TRUE to say that marijuana   30.____

    A. is an aphrodisiac
    B. is addictive
    C. interferes with the thought processes
    D. causes violence and crime

31. The MOST widely misused of all drugs is   31.____

    A. alcohol   B. marijuana
    C. heroin   D. cocaine

32. All of the following concerning heroin are correct EXCEPT it   32.____

    A. is an antispasmodic
    B. is a derivative of opium
    C. is considered a hypnotic rather than a narcotic
    D. has mild, pain relieving powers

33. All of the following associations are correct EXCEPT	33.____

    A. narcotic–novocaine
    B. barbiturate–luminal
    C. stimulant–amphetamine
    D. sedative–benzedrine

34. Alcohol supplies to the body	34.____

    A. minerals   B. protein
    C. calories   D. none of these

35. All of the following statements concerning alcohol are correct EXCEPT:	35.____

    A. The effects of alcohol upon the brain are not felt until the alcohol begins to get into the bloodstream.
    B. While alcohol is absorbed quickly by the body, it is eliminated slowly.
    C. The metabolism of alcohol in the body is speeded up by increased activity.
    D. The stomach cannot change alcohol.

KEY (CORRECT ANSWERS)

1. B	11. C	21. B
2. C	12. D	22. B
3. C	13. B	23. B
4. D	14. B	24. C
5. B	15. A	25. A
6. A	16. C	26. B
7. B	17. D	27. C
8. D	18. A	28. B
9. D	19. D	29. D
10. B	20. C	30. C
	31. A	
	32. C	
	33. D	
	34. C	
	35. C	

EXAMINATION SECTION
TEST 1

DIRECTIONS: Each question or incomplete statement is followed by several suggested answers or completions. Select the one that BEST answers the question or completes the statement. *PRINT THE LETTER OF THE CORRECT ANSWER IN THE SPACE AT THE RIGHT.*

1. The fact is that alcohol

    A. stimulates driving alertness when sleep is needed
    B. is a depressant
    C. has no caloric value
    D. affects all persons in the same degree

    1.____

2. The fallacy is that alcohol

    A. slows reaction time
    B. has no mineral value
    C. is an anesthetic
    D. cures a cold

    2.____

3. The CORRECT regimen for an alcoholic is to

    A. drink less gradually
    B. drink just before meals
    C. stop drinking alcohol beverages completely
    D. drink only at home

    3.____

4. In the brain, excessive alcohol acts as a(n)

    A. stimulant
    B. anaesthetic
    C. readily available fuel
    D. vitamin-carrier

    4.____

5. The trend toward alcoholism is MOST often

    A. a symptom of personality maladjustment
    B. caused by heredity
    C. associated with the sex of the individual
    D. associated with the individual's occupation

    5.____

6. Excessive intake of alcoholic beverages over a period of time

    A. hampers the production of gastric juice
    B. reduces nervous anxiety
    C. increases mental alertness
    D. dilates the blood vessels

    6.____

7. Today, the nature of general clinical treatment of alcoholism is

   A. group psychotherapy
   B. incarceration
   C. tapering off and substitution
   D. physiotherapy

8. An ounce of alcohol (95%) has an APPROXIMATE caloric value of

   A. 200   B. 300   C. 400   D. 500

9. *Alcoholics Anonymous* was organized by

   A. alcoholic addicts
   B. the federal government
   C. private organizations
   D. the American Medical Association

10. It is believed that atabuse

    A. sensitizes humans against alcohol
    B. forms an unstable compound with alcohol
    C. stimulates the gag reflex
    D. promotes elimination of alcohol from the body

11. Excessive alcohol intake ultimately

    A. stimulates body reactions
    B. accelerates mental alertness
    C. depresses
    D. lowers body resistance to infections

12. The malnutrition associated with alcoholism USUALLY results from

    A. impaired digestion
    B. disturbed metabolism
    C. excessive craving for proteins
    D. reduction in diet essentials

13. Excessive use of alcohol is indulged in because it is believed to

    A. quiet the nerves
    B. stimulate brain action
    C. relieve emotional tension
    D. overcome social inadequacy

14. Alcohol FIRST affects

    A. judgment   B. memory
    C. muscular coordination   D. control of speech

15. To the nervous system, alcohol acts as a   15.____

    A. stimulant   B. depressant
    C. gratifier   D. agitator

16. Characteristic symptoms of chronic alcoholism include   16.____

    A. damage to brain tissue
    B. increase in weight
    C. exsiccosis
    D. periods of depression

17. The anesthetizing action of alcohol FIRST affects the exercise of   17.____

    A. muscular coordination   B. control of speech
    C. judgment   D. memory

18. Acute intoxication may properly be labeled a psychosis because it involves   18.____

    A. severe loss of contact with reality
    B. emotional inadequacies
    C. intellectual limitations
    D. bodily as well as mental disease

19. The treatment of alcoholic pellagra is a balanced diet AND   19.____

    A. penicillin injections
    B. oral antibiotics
    C. thiamin injections
    D. amytal injections

20. *Cured* alcoholics   20.____

    A. can control the amount they drink
    B. cannot ever *drink normally*
    C. need moral help to drink within *normal limits*
    D. can drink some alcohol as long as they eat with it

21. Alcohol is MOST often used excessively in order to   21.____

    A. induce sleep
    B. stimulate brain action
    C. overcome social inadequacy
    D. furnish temporary release from tensions

22. To cure drug addiction, the A.M.A. believes that the BEST procedure is to   22.____

    A. maintain stable dosages in addicts
    B. furnish narcotics at no cost
    C. establish withdrawal clinics
    D. give constant control in a drug–free environment

23. Of the following, the MOST dangerous of the narcotic poisons is 23.____
    A. codeine   B. opium   C. heroin   D. marijuana

24. Statistics indicate that MOST youngsters start the drug habit with 24.____
    A. marijuana   B. heroin   C. cocaine   D. morphine

25. Alcohol is a 25.____
    A. stimulant   B. narcotic   C. depressant   D. none of these

KEY (CORRECT ANSWERS)

1. B	11. C
2. D	12. D
3. C	13. C
4. B	14. A
5. A	15. B
6. A	16. D
7. A	17. C
8. A	18. A
9. A	19. C
10. A	20. B

21. D
22. D
23. C
24. A
25. C

TEST 2

DIRECTIONS: Each question or incomplete statement is followed by several suggested answers or completions. Select the one that BEST answers the question or completes the statement. *PRINT THE LETTER OF THE CORRECT ANSWER IN THE SPACE AT THE RIGHT.*

1. In general, of the following, the MOST effective cure of addiction to drugs is   1.____

    A. sustained medical treatment
    B. change of occupation
    C. voluntary tapering off of the use of drugs
    D. conquering the habit by will power

2. The method used to train teenagers in the control of narcotic habits in a school on Ward's Island is the   2.____

    A. penal colony
    B. strict regulatory
    C. clinical examination control
    D. permissive

3. A drug which is a substitute for morphine in the treatment of drug addiction is   3.____

    A. codeine   B. demerol   C. pantapon   D. methadone

4. An hypnotic drug which does NOT initiate drug addiction is   4.____

    A. dormison   B. sodium amytal
    C. sodium phenobarbital   D. seconal

5. The MOST harmful drug derived from opium is   5.____

    A. heroin   B. morphine   C. cocaine   D. codeine

6. The MOST recent statistics indicate that, of the following, the leading cause of accidental deaths from poisoning is   6.____

    A. morphine   B. narcotine
    C. barbituates   D. lead

7. Marijuana is made from   7.____

    A. opium   B. codeine
    C. hemp leaves D. cocoa

8. To a drug addict, reefer or joint mean   8.____

    A. cigarettes   B. powders
    C. capsules   D. pills

9. *Goofballs* used by drug addicts contained   9.____

    A. chloral   B. hyoscyamine
    C. stramonium   D. barbituric acid

10. Recent statistics indicate that MOST youngsters start the drug habit with   10.____

    A. marijuana   B. heroin   C. cocaine   D. morphine

11. Recent information regarding cocaine indicates that it

    A. is purely recreational
    B. is highly addictive
    C. is helpful in reducing stress and hypertension
    D. should be used only prescribed by a physician

12. A habit-forming drug is

    A. sulfathiozole   B. quinidine
    C. demerol   D. potassium acetate

13. Usually, the FIRST step to drugs by a youngster is a

    A. deck   B. snort   C. reefer   D. cap

14. Preventing unlawful trade in narcotics is assigned to

    A. Drug Authority
    B. Bureau of Narcotics
    C. Bureau of Customs
    D. United Nations Commission on Narcotic Drugs

15. *Tolerance* in drug addiction means the amount that

    A. quiets the nerves
    B. produces unconsciousness
    C. can be taken without character changes
    D. produces the desired effect

16. Marijuana is obtained from the

    A. hemp plant   B. thorn apple
    C. cocoa shrub   D. nightshade plant

17. According to the authorities, relationship between the incidence of cancer and smoking is

    A. controversial   B. negative
    C. positive   D. incidental

18. The responsibility for preventing unlawful domestic trade in narcotics rests with the

    A. United Nations Commission on Narcotics
    B. Bureau of Customs, U.S. Treasury Department
    C. Drug Enforcement Agency (DEA), U.S. Treasury Department
    D. United States Drug Authority, Legal Division

19. In addicts, drug withdrawal symptoms include vomiting and changes in

    A. A. pupils of the eyes
    B. muscular control
    C. color of the skin
    D. color of the whites of the eyeballs

20. If a teacher discovers a pupil who is taking drugs, she should report it to the   20._____

    A. dean or assistant principal
    B. police
    C. principal of the school
    D. pupil's parents

21. In addicts, a moderate drug abstinence syndrome is characterized by   21._____

    A. fever, increased blood pressure, insominia, acute restlessness, and rapid breathing
    B. depression, excessive perspiration, and yawning
    C. inertia, body tremors, and fits of sneezing
    D. diarrhea, chills, and depression

22. Opium is derived from   22._____

    A. hemp fiber   B. nightshade plant
    C. poppy   D. ragweed

23. A *mainliner* is a drug addict who uses the drug for   23._____

    A. intra-muscular injection
    B. snorting
    C. smoking
    D. intra-venal injection

24. Prolonged administration of narcotics is MOST likely to result in   24._____

    A. addiction
    B. reduced physical resistance
    C. increased aggressiveness
    D. need for a change in prescription

25. A plant from which peyote is obtained is the   25._____

    A. nightshade plant   B. fox glove
    C. gentian   D. mescal catcus

26. *Half-way house* is the name of a(n)   26._____

    A. dual purpose house providing facilities for living as well as conducting a business
    B. nursing home for terminal care of cancer patients
    C. rehabilitation center for ex-drug addicts and patients released from mental hospitals
    D. nursing home for senile aged persons

27. To avoid detection, the heroin addict injects the 27.____

    A. nasal mucosa and the gums
    B. gums and the vagina
    C. nasal mucosa and the vagina
    D. conjunctiva

28. A highly dangerous and addictive synthetic narcotic is 28.____

    A. amidol   B. amidone
    C. cobalamine   D. pyridoxine

29. During the 1993-1997 term of President Clinton, drug use by young people 29.____

    A. remained steady
    B. increased by one million
    C. declined
    D. cannot be statistically determined

30. A POSITIVE effect of decriminalizing drug use by medical administration would be 30.____

    A. fewer addicts
    B. increased medical costs
    C. less drug-related crime
    D. making drug use more acceptable

KEY (CORRECT ANSWERS)

1.	A	11.	B	21.	A
2.	D	12.	C	22.	C
3.	D	13.	C	23.	D
4.	A	14.	B	24.	A
5.	A	15.	D	25.	D
6.	C	16.	A	26.	C
7.	C	17.	C	27.	B
8.	A	18.	C	28.	B
9.	D	19.	A	29.	B
10.	A	20.	C	30.	C

EXAMINATION SECTION
TEST 1

DIRECTIONS: Each question or incomplete statement is followed by several suggested answers or completions. Select the one that BEST answers the question or completes the statement. *PRINT THE LETTER OF THE CORRECT ANSWER IN THE SPACE AT THE RIGHT.*

1. Research indicates that among the following psychological factors, the one most likely to increase an individual's potential for substance dependence is a(n) 1.____

    A. internal locus of control
    B. *Type A* personality
    C. high feeling of self-worth
    D. tendency toward risk-seeking behavior

2. Of the following substances, the use of_____ is most clearly linked to violent crime. 2.____

    A. marijuana
    B. alcohol
    C. LSD
    D. heroin

3. The neurotransmitter that is inhibited by sedative hypnotics is 3.____

    A. GABA
    B. dopamine
    C. acetylcholine
    D. serotonin

4. At moderate doses, stimulants can produce 4.____

    A. paranoia
    B. a sense of well-being
    C. a dreamy/sleepy state
    D. a loss of inhibitions

5. *Chipping* is a term that refers to the attempt to distribute lower doses of_____ at intervals that will avoid addiction. 5.____

    A. heroin
    B. marijuana
    C. cocaine
    D. alcohol

6. Amphetamines 6.____

    A. can cause panic, agitation, hallucinations, and paranoid delusions
    B. generally increase appetite and decrease fatigue
    C. block the reception of dopamine in the nervous system
    D. cause a period of depression and fatigue that is usually followed by feelings of euphoria

15

7. A person who is designated as a *Type 2* alcoholic has 7._____

   A. comorbid diabetes
   B. developed the disease early in life
   C. limited mobility
   D. a pronounced serotonin deficit in the brain

8. A common model of substance abuse has the person beginning with beer, wine, or cigarettes, and then moving on to hard liquor and marijuana, and subsequently to other illicit drugs. This progression is known as 8._____

   A. the tolerance curve
   B. situational use
   C. staging
   D. compulsion

9. The most appropriate goal of drug education programs is to 9._____

   A. relay information
   B. screen for likely drug users
   C. modify pre-addictive behaviors
   D. gather information from attendants

10. The primary factor in the decline in alcohol use among high school students from 1980 to the first decade of the 21st century was 10._____

    A. a trickle-down effect from the decline in alcohol use among college students
    B. a decline in binge drinking
    C. an increase in the use of illicit drugs
    D. less accessibility to alcohol

11. The most widely prescribed class of drugs in the United States is 11._____

    A. steroids
    B. barbiturates
    C. opiates
    D. benzodiazepines

12. The most likely cause of death among heavy users of alcohol is 12._____

    A. cardiovascular disease
    B. cirrhosis of the liver
    C. digestive disorders
    D. vehicular accidents

13. Cocaethylene, a dangerous drug metabolite, is produced by the combination of cocaine and 13._____

    A. alcohol
    B. heroin
    C. marijuana
    D. LSD

14. _____ is a central nervous system depressant.

   A. Heroin
   B. Marijuana
   C. Cocaine
   D. Alcohol

15. The main reason for the lengthy amount of time it takes to metabolize and excrete marijuana is that it is

   A. excreted only by the lungs
   B. stored in fat cells for up to several weeks after each use
   C. an inhaled particulate, rather than a liquid or solid
   D. one of the main components in renal calculi (kidney stones)

16. Among problem drinkers, the personality characteristic that is MOST likely to be shared is

   A. personal maladjustment
   B. depression
   C. emotional immaturity
   D. sexual dysfunction or deviance

17. Which of the following is a prominent SSRI (selective serotonin reuptake inhibitor) drug?

   A. Miltown
   B. Valium
   C. Darvon
   D. Prozac

18. Alcohol begins to influence the brain, vision, and decision-making at a blood alcohol concentration (BAC) of about

   A. 0.01
   B. 0.02
   C. 0.04
   D. 0.08

19. _____ is a term that refers to the violent behavior that results from the conflict inherent in the drug trade.

   A. Transferred intent
   B. Global wave
   C. Systemic link
   D. Collateral damage

20. The _____ theory of substance dependence holds that eventually, the vicious cycle develops in which the motivation for drug taking shifts from a desire for the euphoric high to the need to relive an increasingly intense *down* feeling that follows drug use.

   A. moral weakness
   B. circular reasoning
   C. gateway
   D. opponent-process

21. When compared to other routes of administration, drugs administered _____ are generally absorbed more slowly.

    A. by intravenous injection
    B. by intramuscular injection
    C. orally
    D. by inhalation

22. The substance_____ is used to treat overdose from heroin and other opioids by blocking the receptors that normally bind with the drug.

    A. naloxone
    B. clonidine
    C. disulfiram
    D. methadone

23. The antipsychotic drug chlorpromazine (Thorazine) is sometimes used to block the effects of each of the following, EXCEPT

    A. psilocybin
    B. mescaline
    C. PCP
    D. LSD

24. The neurotransmitter_____ is a primary agent in the *pleasure pathway* in the brain, which is believed to be involved in substance dependence.

    A. dopamine
    B. norepinephrine
    C. serotonin
    D. acetylcholine

25. Alcohol withdrawal symptoms can include
    I. convulsions
    II. insomnia
    III. tremors
    IV. hallucinations

    A. I, II and III
    B. II only
    C. II and III
    D. I, II, III and IV

KEY (CORRECT ANSWERS)

1.	D	11.	D
2.	B	12.	D
3.	A	13.	A
4.	A	14.	D
5.	A	15.	B
6.	A	16.	A
7.	B	17.	D
8.	C	18.	B
9.	A	19.	C
10.	D	20.	D

21. C
22. A
23. C
24. A
25. D

TEST 2

DIRECTIONS: Each question or incomplete statement is followed by several suggested answers or completions. Select the one that BEST answers the question or completes the statement. *PRINT THE LETTER OF THE CORRECT ANSWER IN THE SPACE AT THE RIGHT.*

1. The medical approach to alcoholism, which views it as a disease, also holds that the only acceptable goal is   1.____

   A. a lifetime prescription of Antabuse
   B. total abstinence
   C. controlled social drinking with trusted friends and family members
   D. inpatient confinement

2. Which of the following is NOT a typical symptom of alcohol withdrawal?   2.____

   A. Sweating
   B. Irritability
   C. Flushed skin
   D. Depression

3. In the human brain, a respiratory center necessary for breathing is located in the   3.____

   A. hindbrain
   B. cerebellum
   C. medulla
   D. thalamus

4. _____ prevention programs are designed to prevent substance dependence before it begins.   4.____

   A. Primary
   B. Secondary
   C. Tertiary
   D. Quaternary

5. Which of the following is NOT a synthetic opiate?   5.____

   A. Fentanyl
   B. Morphine
   C. Methadone
   D. Meperidine

6. Benzodiazepines are prescribed primarily to treat   6.____

   A. substance dependence
   B. depression
   C. anxiety
   D. pain

7. The area of the brain most effected by tetrahydrocannabinol (THC) is the   7.____

   A. hippocampus
   B. hypothalamus
   C. cerebrum
   D. medulla

8. The primary feature of substance abuse is the 8._____

   A. usage of increasing amounts to achieve the same high
   B. feeling of a need for the substance
   C. use of the substance in order to prevent withdrawal
   D. continued use of a substance despite risks or problems in living

9. Currently, methaqualone is a Schedule _____ drug. 9._____

   A. I
   B. II
   C. III
   D. IV

10. Among the elderly, the most common trigger event for excessive drinking is 10._____

    A. crime victimization
    B. retirement
    C. the death of a spouse
    D. the death of a child

11. Which of the following is a benzodiazepine? 11._____

    A. Placidyl
    B. Nembutal
    C. Valium
    D. Miltown

12. Clinically, opioids 12._____

    A. stimulate awareness
    B. have no medically recognized use
    C. increase appetite
    D. relieve pain

13. Alcoholic dementia is associated with 13._____

    A. an enlargement of the brain ventricles
    B. liver damage
    C. a permanent reduction in acetylcholine receptors
    D. a damaged hypothalamus

14. Which of the following factors is LEAST likely to result in a decrease in the intoxicating effect of a drug? 14._____

    A. concurrent intake of food
    B. increase in body fat stores
    C. greater body mass
    D. fewer body fat stores

15. Generally, the most dangerous combination of substances occurs with   15.____

    A. alcohol and marijuana
    B. alcohol and sedative hypnotics
    C. hallucinogens and narcotics
    D. amphetamines and sedative hypnotics

16. Which of the following is a risk factor for alcoholism?   16.____

    A. Not completing high school
    B. Being male
    C. Being African-American
    D. Being married

17. The route of administration that puts a drug into the layer of fat directly beneath the skin is   17.____

    A. inunction
    B. transdermal injection
    C. intramuscular injection
    D. subcutaneous injection

18. Which of the following is NOT an immediate effect of nitrous oxide?   18.____

    A. Euphoria
    B. Dehydration
    C. Cardiac arrhythmia
    D. Spontaneous laughter

19. LSD research has demonstrated that   19.____

    A. it is physiologically addictive
    B. tolerance is acquired rapidly
    C. it is absorbed slowly through the GI tract
    D. it is taken up selectively by the brain

20. In adulthood, the factor that is most closely linked to the onset of alcoholism is   20.____

    A. peer relations
    B. ethnic identity
    C. family history of alcoholism
    D. socioeconomic status

21. A primary duty of the federal Drug Enforcement Agency (DEA) is to   21.____

    A. enforce federal laws related to illicit narcotic drugs and cooperating with state and local agencies in the enforcement of state narcotics laws
    B. conduct drug abuse prevention programs
    C. gather intelligence on traffickers in illicit drugs
    D. regulate the flow and manufacture of legal but controlled drugs

22. At moderate doses, opiates can produce   22.____

    A. hypertension
    B. hypothermia
    C. respiratory depression
    D. constricted pupils

23. For most alcoholics, the first step in treatment is   23.____

    A. the first of the Twelve Steps
    B. detoxification
    C. individual therapy
    D. inpatient admission

24. *Club drugs* often used by young adults at all-night dance parties or at dance clubs and bars, include each of the following, EXCEPT   24.____

    A. ketamine
    B. GHB (gamma hydroxybutyrate)
    C. marijuana
    D. MDMA (ecstasy)

25. The most widely used opiate antagonist in withdrawal treatment is   25.____

    A. methadone
    B. clonidine
    C. chlorpromazine
    D. naltrexone

KEY (CORRECT ANSWERS)

1. B
2. C
3. C
4. A
5. B

6. C
7. A
8. D
9. A
10. C

11. C
12. D
13. A
14. D
15. B

16. B
17. D
18. B
19. B
20. C

21. D
22. B
23. B
24. C
25. D

TEST 3

DIRECTIONS: Each question or incomplete statement is followed by several suggested answers or completions. Select the one that BEST answers the question or completes the statement. *PRINT THE LETTER OF THE CORRECT ANSWER IN THE SPACE AT THE RIGHT.*

1. Which of the following sedative hypnotics is neither a barbiturate nor a benzodiazepine? 1._____

   A. Methaqualone
   B. Chlorazepate
   C. Diazepam
   D. Secobarbital

2. A substance that effectively increases the activity of a neurotransmitter by binding with a cell receptor and causing a response is known as a(n) 2._____

   A. barbiturate
   B. narcotic
   C. agonist
   D. analgesic

3. Which of the following is an opioid, developed for pharmaceutical use in the 1990s, which has proven to be addictive for many users? 3._____

   A. OxyContin
   B. Fen-Phen
   C. Tamgesic
   D. St. John's wort

4. Which of the following routes of administration greatly increases a drug user's risk for hepatitis and AIDS? 4._____

   A. Inhalation
   B. Ingestion (oral)
   C. Parenteral (injection)
   D. Topical (absorption through the skin)

5. The form of cannabis with the weakest concentration of tetrahydrocan-nabinol (THC) is 5._____

   A. marijuana
   B. sinsemilla
   C. hashish
   D. hashish oil

6. Each year, about 75 percent of the drug-related deaths in the United States are associated with 6._____

   A. alcohol
   B. polydrug episodes
   C. narcotics
   D. cocaine

7. The drug most often abused by adolescents is marijuana, followed by 7._____

   A. cocaine
   B. MDMA (ecstasy)
   C. barbiturates
   D. inhalants

8. What is the term for the interaction that takes place when two drugs are mixed together to produce a greater effect than that of either drug taken separately? 8._____

   A. Antagonism
   B. Potentiation
   C. Pronunciation
   D. Agonism

9. The oxidative rate-the rate at which the body metabolizes a substance-for alcohol in adults is a little under 9._____

   A. one drink per hour
   B. two drinks per hour
   C. three drinks in two hours
   D. four drinks per day

10. Which of the following is a common side effect associated with the use of antidepressant drugs, especially tricyclics (Elavil) and Serotonin and norepinephrine reuptake inhibitors (SNRIs)? 10._____

    A. Sweating
    B. Blotchy skin
    C. Constipation
    D. Ruid retention

11. _____ programs are designed to minimize the physiological changes associated with withdrawal from a substance. 11._____

    A. Withdrawal
    B. Therapeutic community
    C. 12-step
    D. Milieu

12. The most widely used sedative hypnotic drug is 12._____

    A. Seconal
    B. alcohol
    C. diazepam
    D. methaqualone

13. Of all Americans who complete a drug treatment program, the percentage who remain drug-free for at least a year afterward is about 13._____

    A. 5-10
    B. 15-35
    C. 30-50
    D. 60-80

14. *Speedball* is a street term that refers to the combination of

    A. methamphetamine and heroin
    B. cocaine and heroin
    C. cocaine and methamphetamine
    D. methamphetamine and LSD

15. Neurotransmitters are synthesized and metabolized in the body by

    A. enzymes
    B. amino acids
    C. axons
    D. metabolites

16. A substance that produces vivid sensory awareness or feelings of increased insight is said to have _____ properties.

    A. hallucinogenic
    B. psychedelic
    C. barbiturate
    D. narcotic

17. Which of the following is NOT a fundamental process associated with the concept of addiction?

    A. Reinforcement
    B. Tolerance
    C. Physical dependence
    D. Affective disorder

18. Blood alcohol concentration (BAC) becomes lethal at about

    A. 0.2
    B. 0.4
    C. 0.8
    D. 1.0

19. Which of the following is a common side effect of antipsychotic drugs?

    A. Photosensitivity
    B. Excitability
    C. Alzheimer's disease
    D. Constipation

20. Nembutal and Seconal are

    A. opiates
    B. barbiturates
    C. benzodiazepines
    D. stimulants

21. Of the following, the substance that causes the greatest overall damage to human tissue is

    A. marijuana
    B. LSD
    C. cocaine
    D. alcohol

22. Which of the following is NOT used as an alternative to anabolic steroids?

    A. Clonidine
    B. Clenbuterol
    C. GHB (gamma hydroxybutyrate)
    D. Androstenedione

23. The most likely result of drinking excessively before bedtime in order to relax is _____, which may produce anxiety and restlessness.

    A. nightmares
    B. hypertension
    C. dream deficit
    D. sleep deficit

24. Which of the following was originally used as a nasal decongestant?

    A. Cocaine
    B. Amphetamine
    C. Opium
    D. Morphine

25. The phenomenon that most clearly demonstrates that there is a cognitive as well as physiological factor involved in drug reaction and dependence is the

    A. disease model
    B. opponent-process theory
    C. expectancy effect
    D. contingency management

KEY (CORRECT ANSWERS)

1.	A	11.	A
2.	C	12.	B
3.	A	13.	C
4.	C	14.	B
5.	A	15.	A
6.	B	16.	A
7.	D	17.	D
8.	B	18.	B
9.	A	19.	A
10.	C	20.	B

21. D
22. A
23. C
24. B
25. C

TEST 4

DIRECTIONS: Each question or incomplete statement is followed by several suggested answers or completions. Select the one that BEST answers the question or completes the statement. *PRINT THE LETTER OF THE CORRECT ANSWER IN THE SPACE AT THE RIGHT.*

1. The *amotivational syndrome* is a controversial theory that refers to an indifference to long-range plans among habitual users of

    A. alcohol
    B. cocaine
    C. heroin
    D. marijuana

    1.____

2. Which of the following hallucinogens is derived from the peyote cactus?

    A. Mescaline
    B. Psilocybin
    C. Atropine
    D. Harmaline

    2.____

3. Which of the following is NOT an effect associated with the use of anabolic steroids in men?

    A. Increased sex drive
    B. Gynecomastia (breast development)
    C. Hair loss
    D. Increased blood cholesterol

    3.____

4. The most extensively used illicit drug in the United States today is

    A. marijuana
    B. amphetamine
    C. cocaine
    D. anabolic steroids

    4.____

5. The primary area of the brain that is inhibited by alcohol intoxication is the

    A. hippocampus
    B. medulla
    C. cerebrum
    D. hypothalamus

    5.____

6. Generally, the most difficult time in the process of withdrawal from heroin addiction occurs from_____ hours after the last use.

    A. 6 to 12
    B. 12 to 24
    C. 24 to 72
    D. 72 to 96

    6.____

7. Physical dependence on a drug is most closely associated with

    A. escalating use
    B. withdrawal symptoms
    C. missing days of work or school
    D. a strong compulsion to use the drug

8. Which of the following neurotransmitters is released at the somatic neuromuscular junctions?

    A. Dopamine
    B. Epinephrine
    C. Acetylcholine
    D. Serotonin

9. Alcohol's most significant health-related impact occurs in the _____ system.

    A. respiratory
    B. digestive
    C. endocrine
    D. central nervous

10. An effect common to the use of most inhalants is

    A. spontaneous laughter
    B. dizziness
    C. headache
    D. a loss of inhibition

11. Compared to cocaine, the stimulating effects of amphetamines are

    A. about the same in duration and intensity
    B. longer-lasting and more intense
    C. shorter-lasting and more intense
    D. longer-lasting and less intense

12. Drugs that are classified as *psychedelics* because they enhancing perceptive and thought processes of the brain include each of the following, EXCEPT

    A. LSD
    B. psilocybin
    C. mescaline
    D. ketamine

13. A disorder common among alcoholics, caused by vitamin B_1 deficiency and characterized by disorientation, confusion, abnormal eye movements, and amnesia, is _____ syndrome

    A. Ackerman's
    B. Korsakoff's
    C. Tourette's
    D. Reye's

14. The use of which of the following drugs is MOST likely to lead to tolerance or physical dependence?   14.____

    A. PCP (phencyclidine)
    B. Marijuana
    C. Amphetamine
    D. LSD

15. Common symptoms of cocaine abuse include each of the following, EXCEPT   15.____

    A. insomnia
    B. runny nose
    C. constricted pupils
    D. talkativeness

16. Available statistics on drugs and crime in the United States suggest that most narcotic addicts who commit crimes   16.____

    A. commit mostly *victimless* crimes
    B. are under the influence when they commit crimes
    C. began criminal activity after they became addicted
    D. were engaged in criminal activity before they became addicted

17. Most drugs and metabolites are excreted   17.____

    A. in the form of perspiration, saliva, and tears
    B. in the form of air expired by the lungs
    C. by the gallbladder
    D. by the kidneys

18. Which of the following drugs is used to reduce the severity of narcotic withdrawal symptoms?   18.____

    A. Clonidine
    B. Fentanyl
    C. Naltrexone
    D. Hydrocodone

19. Each of the following is a risk factor for alcohol abuse, EXCEPT   19.____

    A. peer relations
    B. a high tolerance for alcohol
    C. family relations
    D. heredity

20. By using alcohol, a person can induce an increased tolerance for Seconal, despite the fact that the user has never taken Seconal before. This is an example of   20.____

    A. distributive effect
    B. a breach in the blood-brain barrier
    C. cross-tolerance
    D. agonism

21. The class of drugs to which Ritalin belongs, and which are now the drugs of choice for treating attention-deficit/hyperactivity disorder, are   21.____

    A. stimulants
    B. depressants
    C. narcotics
    D. sedative hypnotics

22. Of the following substances, which is a narcotic?   22.____

    A. Heroin
    B. Amphetamine
    C. Alcohol
    D. LSD

23. Dexedrine and Benzedrine are commonly abused   23.____

    A. benzodiazepines
    B. amphetamines
    C. narcotics
    D. barbiturates

24. Nationwide, the primary purpose of the Drug Abuse Warning Network (DAWN) is to   24.____

    A. monitor drug-related hospital emergency department (ED) visits and drug-related deaths
    B. establish in-school programs that teach children about the consequences of drug abuse
    C. establish a network of drug treatment centers
    D. monitor the international trade in illicit drugs

25. The third stage of alcoholism, in which there is a loss of control of drinking and occasional binges of heavy drinking, is the _____ stage.   25.____

    A. pre-alcoholic
    B. chronic
    C. prodromal
    D. crucial

KEY (CORRECT ANSWERS)

1. D
2. A
3. A
4. A
5. C

6. C
7. B
8. C
9. D
10. D

11. D
12. D
13. B
14. C
15. C

16. D
17. D
18. A
19. B
20. C

21. A
22. A
23. B
24. A
25. D

EXAMINATION SECTION
TEST 1

DIRECTIONS: Each question or incomplete statement is followed by several suggested answers or completions. Select the one that BEST answers the question or completes the statement. *PRINT THE LETTER OF THE CORRECT ANSWER IN THE SPACE AT THE RIGHT.*

1. Which of the following symptoms, by itself, would NOT signify that a person receiving treatment for alcoholism might undergo a difficult period of withdrawal?

    A. Previous history of seizures or delirium tremens
    B. Ulcers or gastritis
    C. Irritability or depression
    D. Elevated blood pressure or pulse

2. In general, the format and direction of treatment for alcoholics and people dependent upon drugs should

    A. differ in intensity according to the progression of the addiction
    B. be flexible enough not to interfere with the patient's normal living patterns
    C. begin with immediate isolation
    D. remain the same for all patients

3. Which of the following words is NOT typically used to describe the disease of alcoholism?

    A. Chronic   B. Nonfatal
    C. Primary   D. Hereditary

4. Each of the following symptoms characterizes stage one in an alcoholic subject's withdrawal process EXCEPT

    A. auditory hallucinations   B. loss of appetite
    C. hand tremors   D. diarrhea

5. During the initial stages of recovery, which of the following vitamin supplements is NOT usually among the most important for the typically malnourished alcoholic subject?

    A. Zinc   B. Calcium
    C. B-complex   D. Vitamin C

6. What is the term for the point in recovery treatment that marks the clearest turning point, and signals that the subject has escaped immediate danger?

    A. Submission   B. Substitution
    C. Surrender   D. Synchronization

7. As a rule, _____ should always be excluded from the team making an intervention into an addicted person's life.

    A. staff members of a treatment facility
    B. people with abuse or addiction problems
    C. the addicted person's professional superiors
    D. members of the religious community

8. Approximately what percentage of untreated alcoholics will eventually experience delirium tremens?

   A. 10%   B. 20%   C. 30%   D. 40%

9. Each of the following is considered to be one of the essential elements in subduing an addiction EXCEPT

   A. total abstinence
   B. firm but compassionate care
   C. nutritional repair
   D. vigorous physical exercise

10. Which of the following stages in the progression to freedom from addiction is considered to be the foundation on which all other elements are dependent?

    A. Spiritual well-being
    B. Mental well-being
    C. Total abstinence
    D. Physical well-being

11. Which of the following is a sign of early-stage addiction in an adolescent?

    A. Increase in tolerance
    B. Legal problems
    C. Changes in appearance
    D. Buying drugs

12. Which of the following is NOT normally included in the description of a *typical* alcoholic in the early stages of treatment?

    A. Withdrawn
    B. Suspicious
    C. Talks loudly
    D. Poorly groomed

13. Which of the following is considered to be an internal enabler for abuse or addiction?

    A. Modeling of use by parents
    B. Approval of use by peers
    C. The removal of deterrent consequences
    D. Rationalization of use

14. Approximately what percentage of alcoholics are heavy caffeine drinkers?

    A. 0-10%   B. 10-15%   C. 45-50%   D. 90-95%

15. Good addiction treatment facilities have all of the following characteristics in common EXCEPT

    A. reliance on psychotherapy
    B. family involvement
    C. introduction and participation in AA or related groups
    D. occupational guidance

16. Which factor in an individual's predisposition to addiction is related to the biological differences between addicts and non-addicts?

    A. Genetic
    B. Constitutional
    C. Psychological
    D. Sociocultural

17. Typically, no detoxifying agents or drugs are used for the detoxification period during treatment for addiction to

    A. alcohol   B. opiates   C. cocaine   D. valium

18. Which of the following elements is considered to be unique to teenage alcoholism or addiction?

    A. Self-centeredness
    B. Peer pressure
    C. Rebelliousness
    D. Fear of life without drugs

19. A component of a comprehensive addiction treatment program that is included in the category of evaluation and assessment is

    A. treating physiological crises
    B. family therapy
    C. addiction screening
    D. stress reduction

20. The middle stages of alcoholism are often characterized by the onset of

    A. a progressive increase in drinking
    B. financial dependence
    C. guilty feelings
    D. alcohol-related arrests

21. Which of the following unconscious defense mechanisms, used by an addicted person, is characterized by blaming others for behaviors and consequences?

    A. Denial   B. Minimization
    C. Rationalization   D. Projection

22. Which of the following *leverages,* or inducements for voluntary submission to treatment, would be LEAST appropriate for use by members of an intervention team?

    A. Termination of employment
    B. Threat of divorce
    C. Threat of institutionalization
    D. Termination of friendship

23. Which of the following is NOT considered to be one of the primary goals in a structured detoxification process?

    A. Helping ease the pain associated with withdrawal
    B. Allowing the symptoms of withdrawal to run their natural course
    C. Correcting underlying medical problems or malnutrition
    D. Preparing patient for abstinence without dependence on other drugs

24. The _____ is ALWAYS a mistake on the part of treatment staff while the patient is going through the detoxification process.

    A. administration of narcotic sedatives
    B. prolonged isolation of the subject
    C. attempt to induce the subject's acknowledgement of his/her addiction
    D. liberal administration of multivitamin supplements

25. The enabling behaviors MOST likely to be practiced by the addicted person's family members in the intermediate stages of addiction are 25.____
    A. cooperation and collaboration
    B. protecting and shielding
    C. codependence and cohabitation
    D. control and guilt

KEY (CORRECT ANSWERS)

1. C
2. D
3. B
4. A
5. A

6. C
7. B
8. A
9. D
10. C

11. A
12. D
13. D
14. D
15. A

16. B
17. C
18. B
19. C
20. C

21. D
22. C
23. B
24. C
25. D

TEST 2

DIRECTIONS: Each question or incomplete statement is followed by several suggested answers or completions. Select the one that BEST answers the question or completes the statement. *PRINT THE LETTER OF THE CORRECT ANSWER IN THE SPACE AT THE RIGHT.*

1. Recurring withdrawal symptoms are LEAST common during the treatment for _____ addiction.

    A. alcohol B. valium C. amphetamine D. cocaine

2. The normalization process during the posttreatment restructuring phase of recovery treatment includes

    A. increasing self-esteem through feedback
    B. learning communication skills
    C. a physical exercise program
    D. implementation of a healthy diet

3. Stage three in an alcoholic's withdrawal process is characterized by

    A. delirium tremens   B. seizures
    C. auditory hallucinations   D. insomnia

4. The characteristic of an addicted person's recovery illustrated by the person's acknowledgement of his/her addiction is termed

    A. surrender B. acceptance C. admission D. restitution

5. During the early stages of recovery treatment, which of the following characteristics of a subject's expression or demeanor is usually NOT a cause for worry on the part of the treatment staff?

    A. Boredom B. Anxiety C. Aloofness D. Arrogance

6. Which of the following steps should be taken FIRST by friends/family members who want to practice intervention in a person's addiction?

    A. Devising a treatment plan
    B. Confronting the addicted person
    C. Getting help for the person's family
    D. Asking others for help

7. An addicted person who would require one of the less intense levels of recovery treatment and care would PROBABLY

    A. have chronic psychiatric problems
    B. lack family or social support
    C. already be resigned to treatment
    D. have family members who were also addicted

8. The percentage of people with psychotic disorders among the alcoholic population is _____ that of the general population.

    A. half as much as   B. no different than
    C. one a half times as much as D. twice as much as

9. A recovering addict will typically experience the GREATEST risk of relapse during

   A. detoxification
   B. the first six months of treatment
   C. the second six months of treatment
   D. late stage recovery

10. The depressant which usually carries the GREATEST potential for dependency or abuse is

    A. valium   B. librium   C. halcion   D. seconal

11. Each of the following is considered to be a crucial element in the detoxification process EXCEPT

    A. stimulation   B. security   C. supplements   D. sedation

12. Which of the addiction risk factors is considered to be the MOST influential?

    A. Hereditary   B. Behavioral   C. Demographic   D. Psychiatric

13. The component of a, comprehensive addiction treatment program that is included in the category of medical and psychiatric management is

    A. detoxification
    B. recreation and leisure
    C. group therapy
    D. relapse prevention training

14. Which of the following is NOT typically a characteristic more pronounced in female alcoholics than in males?

    A. Greater degree of guilt
    B. More likely to feel locked into unhealthy relationships
    C. More likely to use illegal drugs
    D. More difficulty dealing with feelings of inadequacy

15. The information needed first to determine whether a person is addicted, and to which all other factors are secondary considerations, are the

    A. results of the person's physical examination
    B. person's performance level at home and on the job
    C. person's overall pattern of alcohol or drug use
    D. person's family medical history

16. Which of the following is considered part of the necessary treatment for an alcoholic subject who has entered stage one of the withdrawal process?

    A. Sedation
    B. Well-lit room
    C. Constant medical supervision
    D. Intravenous administration of fluid supplements

17. Mood-altering drugs are capable of each of the following EXCEPT 17.____

    A. causing psychiatric symptoms of varying intensity
    B. masking existing psychiatric symptoms and disorders
    C. curing certain psychiatric disorders
    D. initiate or worsen existing psychiatric disorders

18. When initially questioning a subject about his or her use of alcohol or drugs, the questioner should avoid asking, until the later stages of treatment, whether 18.____

    A. the subject drinks or uses drugs
    B. the subject has experienced any trouble related to the use of drugs or alcohol
    C. the subject feels any guilt about his/her use of drugs or alcohol
    D. any friends or relatives have had problems with drugs or alcohol

19. Elderly alcoholics typically differ from others in that they are MORE likely to 19.____

    A. deny their addiction
    B. combine their alcoholism with over-the-counter drug addiction
    C. begin their drinking in social settings
    D. become afflicted with alcoholism

20. The normalization process during the mature recovery phase of treatment includes 20.____

    A. personality restructuring
    B. introduction of normal sleep patterns
    C. personality growth
    D. stress reduction techniques

21. Which of the following is a sign that an adolescent has entered the intermediate stage of addiction? 21.____

    A. Denial
    B. Abuse as an act of defiance
    C. Increasing tolerance
    D. First blackouts

22. Which of the following is NOT one of the benefits associated with the use of sedatives during a subject's withdrawal period? 22.____

    A. Reduces fear of new surroundings and circumstances
    B. Shortens the time needed for detoxification
    C. Reduces likelihood of premature departure
    D. Prevents progression of withdrawal symptoms into advanced stages

23. Which stage in the progression to freedom from addiction is considered to be the intermediate level of recovery? 23.____

    A. Spiritual well-being   B. Mental well-being
    C. Total abstinence   D. Physical well-being

24. Each of the following symptoms typically signify that a drinker has progressed to the advanced stages of the alcoholic disease EXCEPT   24._____

    A. lack of attention to hygiene
    B. increased tolerance for alcohol
    C. morning drinking
    D. alcohol-related accidents

25. What is the typical percentage of alcoholic people entering treatment programs who will require the use of sedatives during withdrawal?   25._____

    A. 1-10% B. 10-20% C. 20-30% D. 30-40%

KEY (CORRECT ANSWERS)

1.	A	11.	A
2.	A	12.	A
3.	A	13.	A
4.	C	14.	C
5.	B	15.	C
6.	D	16.	B
7.	C	17.	C
8.	B	18.	C
9.	B	19.	B
10.	D	20.	A

21. A
22. B
23. B
24. B
25. C

EXAMINATION SECTION
TEST 1

DIRECTIONS: Each question or incomplete statement is followed by several suggested answers or completions. Select the one that BEST answers the question or completes the statement. *PRINT THE LETTER OF THE CORRECT ANSWER IN THE SPACE AT THE RIGHT.*

1. Which of the following is NOT an inherent characteristic of addiction? 1.____

   A. Tolerance changes
   B. Dissolution of relationships
   C. Physiological dependence
   D. Loss of self-control

2. Which type of factor in an individual's predisposition to addiction has the GREATEST potential to increase the risk of addiction after exposure to a substance? 2.____

   A. Genetic   B. Constitutional   C. Psychological   D. Sociocultural

3. The enabling behavior MOST likely practiced by the addicted person's family members in the early stages of addiction are 3.____

   A. cooperation and collaboration
   B. protecting and shielding
   C. codependence and cohabitation
   D. control and guilt

4. When making initial inquiries about an addicted person's drug or alcohol abuse patterns and history, which of the following is probably the LEAST reliable? 4.____

   A. Information provided by the subject's friends and relatives
   B. Information provided by the patient or subject
   C. Medical histories of subject's family members
   D. Subject's medical record

5. Which of the following is NOT one of the physical factors influencing addiction? 5.____

   A. Heredity
   B. Brain chemistry
   C. Metabolism
   D. Race

6. In a recovery treatment center, which of the following behaviors or characteristics gives the STRONGEST indication that a subject is still addicted? 6.____

   A. Feeling caged or jailed
   B. Mood swings
   C. Nervousness
   D. Depression

7. Which of the following is NOT true of *leverages* used by members of an intervention team to induce an addicted person to voluntarily submit to treatment? They should 7.____

   A. only be used as a last resort
   B. not be carried out if they will result in isolating the addicted person
   C. be agreed upon and supported by every member of the intervention team
   D. not be threatened unless they will definitely be implemented

8. What percentage of untreated alcoholics will eventually experience seizures? 8.____
   A. 5-15%   B. 20-30%   C. 40-50%   D. 55-75%

9. Which of the following is a sign that an adolescent has entered the late stages of addiction? 9.____
   A. Impulsiveness
   B. Decrease in attention span
   C. Chronic depression
   D. Denial

10. The type of drug dependency requiring the longest treatment time is USUALLY caused by 10.____
    A. alcohol
    B. amphetamines
    C. opiates or cocaine
    D. hallucinogens

11. Which of the following is NOT one of the primary factors in the formula that results in addiction? 11.____
    A. Drug effect
    B. Social constraints
    C. Predisposition for abuse
    D. Enabling factors

12. Drugs sometimes used in detoxification and which occupy a person's opiate-receptor sites without creating an accompanying sense of euphoria or loss of consciousness are 12.____
    A. opioids
    B. opiates
    C. agonists
    D. placebos

13. The normalization process during the late recovery phase of treatment includes 13.____
    A. increasingly sobriety-centered lifestyle
    B. discussion of drug hunger
    C. personality growth
    D. stress reduction techniques

14. Which of the following unconscious defense mechanisms, used by an addicted person, is characterized by partial awareness of the severity of the addiction? 14.____
    A. Denial
    B. Minimization
    C. Rationalization
    D. Isolation

15. The characteristic of an addicted person's recovery illustrated by the person's attempt to repair the relationships damaged by his/her addiction is 15.____
    A. fellowship
    B. surrender
    C. admission
    D. restitution

16. Which of the following is a sign that a drinker has entered the late stages of alcoholism? 16.____
    A. Progressive increase in drinking
    B. Broken promises to friends and family
    C. Personality changes
    D. Malnutrition

17. An alcoholic subject is said to have entered stage four of the withdrawal process if he or she experiences

   A. seizures
   B. delirium tremens
   C. vomiting
   D. hallucinations

18. Which of the following unconscious defense mechanisms, used by an addicted person, is characterized by an avoidance of feelings through focusing on logic?

   A. Rationalization
   B. Intellectualization
   C. Repression
   D. Projection

19. Measuring from the starting point of detoxification, what is typically the amount of time required for a recovering person to regain the level of health and well-being associated with his/her pre-addiction lifestyle?

   A. 6 months   B. 1 year   C. 18 months   D. 3 years

20. A characteristic that typically differentiates teenage alcoholism from adult alcoholism is that teenagers

   A. are more likely to explain that they drink to celebrate or be sociable
   B. have a more difficult time with recovery
   C. claim drinking as an escape from life's problems
   D. sustain less physiological damage

21. Which type of recovery treatment is reserved for the most advanced cases of addiction?

   A. Day treatment
   B. Residential treatment
   C. Inpatient hospitalization
   D. Partial hospitalization

22. The use of which opiate drug typically carries the LOWEST risk for dependency or abuse?

   A. Percodan   B. Methadone   C. Codeine   D. Demerol

23. What is the APPROXIMATE mortality rate for alcoholic patients who suffer from delirium tremens?

   A. Zero   B. 1-10%   C. 10-20%   D. 20-30%

24. Addiction is a process influenced primarily by each of the following EXCEPT

   A. factors relating to the individual user
   B. various social factors
   C. factors relating to specific physiological health concerns
   D. factors relating to the drug being used

25. Which of the following statements about alcoholism is NOT true?

   A. Children of alcoholics often learn alcoholic behavior from their parents.
   B. Divorce, loss of a job, death of a loved one, and other life traumas can cause alcoholism.
   C. Alcoholism is often a symptom of larger psychological problems.
   D. An alcoholic in the throes of the disease drinks to avoid self-destruction.

KEY (CORRECT ANSWERS)

1.	B	11.	B
2.	A	12.	C
3.	B	13.	C
4.	B	14.	B
5.	D	15.	D
6.	A	16.	D
7.	B	17.	B
8.	A	18.	B
9.	C	19.	C
10.	C	20.	A

21. C
22. C
23. C
24. C
25. D

TEST 2

DIRECTIONS: Each question or incomplete statement is followed by several suggested answers or completions. Select the one that BEST answers the question or completes the statement. *PRINT THE LETTER OF THE CORRECT ANSWER IN THE SPACE AT THE RIGHT.*

1. Age, peers, and status are examples of _____ factors in an individual's predisposition to addiction.

    A. genetic   B. constitutional   C. psychological   D. sociocultural

2. How many days should an alcoholic subject's detoxification process typically last?

    A. 1-10   B. 10-20   C. 20-30   D. 30-40

3. Which of the following is NOT true of the confrontation that takes place between members of an intervention team and an addicted person?
It must

    A. be rehearsed by all team members together
    B. involve quick-thinking people who can formulate responses to unanticipated statements
    C. involve people from a variety of the addicted person's life experiences
    D. be rigidly planned and structured

4. What is the characteristic of an addicted person's recovery illustrated by the person's expression of willingness to accept the help of treatment staff in the recovery process?

    A. Surrender   B. Acceptance   C. Fellowship   D. Restitution

5. In the early stages of an addicted or alcoholic person's recovery, the process of nutritional repair should include each of the following EXCEPT

    A. three good meals a day
    B. total elimination of caffeine intake
    C. three nutritious snacks a day
    D. increasing the amount of sugars in the diet

6. Which of the following stages in the progression to freedom from addiction is considered to be the final stage, at which recovery is complete?

    A. Spiritual well-being   B. Mental well-being
    C. Total abstinence   D. Physical well-being

7. The FIRST goal of recovery treatment is to remedy _____ damage to the addicted person.

    A. social   B. psychological   C. physical   D. spiritual

8. Which of the following steps should be taken LAST by friends/family members who want to practice intervention in a person's addiction?

    A. Devising a treatment plan
    B. Confronting the addicted person
    C. Getting help for the person's family
    D. Asking others for help

9. Each of the following is a disadvantage associated with the use of sedatives during an alcoholic subject's withdrawal EXCEPT that it

   A. increases suspicion and paranoia
   B. conflicts with the *abstinence* goal of detoxification
   C. lengthens the detoxification period
   D. interferes with the subject's alertness and early participation in treatment

10. Which of the following symptoms does addiction MOST commonly share with other chronic, debilitating diseases?

    A. Central nervous system damage
    B. Seizures
    C. Denial
    D. Physiological damage

11. An addicted person who would require one of the more intense levels of recovery treatment and care would PROBABLY have

    A. minor withdrawal symptoms
    B. family members who attend Al-Anon
    C. already be resigned to treatment
    D. already attempted recovery at least once and failed

12. The enabling behavior MOST likely practiced by the addicted person's family members in the advanced stages of addiction is

    A. cooperation   B. protecting
    C. codependence   D. guilt

13. Which of the following is NOT a symptom associated with stage two in an alcoholic subject's withdrawal process?

    A. Rapid heartbeat   B. Hand tremors
    C. Insomnia   D. Seizures

14. During intervention, participants on the intervention team should avoid describing to the addicted person

    A. concerns for the addicted person's health
    B. observed examples of addiction-related incidents
    C. observed consequences of addiction-related incidents
    D. personal assessment of emotional damage inflicted upon the addicted person's relations

15. During recovery, a subject sometimes becomes dependent on a drug that has the same relative effects on the central nervous system as the drug for which the subject is being treated.
    This is known specifically as

    A. substitution   B. cross-addiction
    C. surrender   D. submission

16. During an intervention, which of the following types of statements should be offered to the addicted person by members of the intervention team?

    A. Generalized comments
    B. Judgments
    C. Observations
    D. Opinions

17. Past failures, emotional trauma, and personality defects are examples of _____ factors in an individual's predisposition to addiction.

    A. genetic
    B. constitutional
    C. psychological
    D. sociocultural

18. The normalization process during the restabilization phase of recovery treatment includes

    A. introducing external motivations for recovery
    B. personality restructuring
    C. personality growth
    D. stress reduction techniques

19. Which characteristic typically differs between female and male alcoholics?

    A. Age
    B. Rate of advancement through addictive stages
    C. Likelihood of concurrent addiction to prescription drugs
    D. Professional status

20. Each of the following is an important factor determining the overall effects of addiction on a family EXCEPT

    A. the type of substance used
    B. the sex of addicted parent
    C. existing feelings of nonaddicted family members toward the addicted
    D. where and when substances are used

21. The component of a comprehensive addiction treatment program that is included in the category of psychosocial rehabilitation is

    A. social assessment
    B. treating medical problems
    C. random drug screenings
    D. detoxification

22. Each of the following is considered a warning sign for the onset of alcoholism's early stages EXCEPT

    A. alcohol-related problems
    B. hiding bottles
    C. changes in drinking patterns
    D. preoccupation with alcohol

23. If sedatives are to be used by a subject during the alcoholic withdrawal period, APPROXIMATELY how long is the recommended period for their use?

    A. For the first overnight period
    B. For the first three or four days
    C. Until the subject does not appear to require sedation
    D. Throughout the entire period of detoxification

24. Which of the following is NOT one of the psychological factors influencing addiction? 24._____

    A. Coping mechanisms
    B. Denial
    C. Tolerance changes
    D. Reinforcing factors

25. The characteristic of an addicted person's recovery illustrated by the person's acknowledgement of his/her individual responsibility for recovery is termed 25._____

    A. surrender
    B. acceptance
    C. fellowship
    D. admission

KEY (CORRECT ANSWERS)

1. D
2. A
3. B
4. A
5. D

6. A
7. C
8. B
9. A
10. C

11. D
12. C
13. D
14. D
15. B

16. C
17. C
18. D
19. C
20. A

21. C
22. B
23. B
24. C
25. B

EXAMINATION SECTION
TEST 1

DIRECTIONS: Each question or incomplete statement is followed by several suggested answers or completions. Select the one that BEST answers the question or completes the statement. *PRINT THE LETTER OF THE CORRECT ANSWER IN THE SPACE AT THE RIGHT.*

1. Deviant behavior is a sociological term used to describe behavior which is not in accord with generally accepted standards. This may include juvenile delinquency, adult criminality, mental or physical illness.
   Comparison of normal with deviant behavior is useful to social workers because it

   A. makes it possible to establish watertight behavioral descriptions
   B. provides evidence of differential social behavior which distinguishes deviant from normal behavior
   C. indicates that deviant behavior is of no concern to social workers
   D. provides no evidence that social role is a determinant of behavior

2. Alcoholism may affect an individual client's ability to function as a spouse, parent, worker, and citizen.
   A social worker's MAIN responsibility to a client with a history of alcoholism is to

   A. interpret to the client the causes of alcoholism as a disease syndrome
   B. work with the alcoholic's family to accept him as he is and stop trying to reform him
   C. encourage the family of the alcoholic to accept casework treatment
   D. determine the origins of his particular drinking problem, establish a diagnosis, and work out a treatment plan for him

3. There is a trend to regard narcotic addiction as a form of illness for which the current methods of intervention have not been effective.
   Research on the combination of social, psychological, and physical causes of addiction would indicate that social workers should

   A. oppose hospitalization of addicts in institutions
   B. encourage the addict to live normally at home
   C. recognize that there is no successful treatment for addiction and act accordingly
   D. use the existing community facilities differentially for each addict

4. A study of social relationships among delinquent and non-delinquent youth has shown that

   A. delinquent youth generally conceal their true feelings and maintain furtive social contacts
   B. delinquents are more impulsive and vivacious than law-abiding boys
   C. non-delinquent youths diminish their active social relationships in order to sublimate any anti-social impulses
   D. delinquent and non-delinquent youths exhibit similar characteristics of impulsiveness and vivaciousness

5. The one of the following which is the CHIEF danger of interpreting the delinquent behavior of a child in terms of morality *alone* when attempting to get at its causes is that

    A. this tends to overlook the likelihood that the causes of the child's actions are more than a negation of morality and involve varied symptoms of disturbance
    B. a child's moral outlook toward life and society is largely colored by that of his parents, thus encouraging parent-child conflict
    C. too careful a consideration of the moral aspects of the offense and of the child's needs may often negate the demands of justice in a case
    D. standards of morality may be of no concern to the delinquent and he may not realize the seriousness of his offenses

6. Experts in the field of personnel administration are generally agreed that an employee should not be under the immediate supervision of more than one supervisor. A certain worker, because of an emergency situation, divides his time equally between two limited caseloads on a prearranged time schedule. Each unit has a different supervisor, and the worker performs substantially the same duties in each caseload.
   The above statement is pertinent in this situation CHIEFLY because

    A. each supervisor, feeling that the cases in her unit should have priority, may demand too much of the worker's time
    B. the two supervisors may have different standards of work performance and may prefer different methods of doing the work
    C. the worker works part-time on each caseload and may not have full knowledge or control of the situation in either caseload
    D. the task of evaluating the worker's services will be doubled, with two supervisors instead of one having to rate his work

7. Experts in modern personnel management generally agree that employees on all job levels should be permitted to offer suggestions for improving work methods.
   Of the following, the CHIEF limitation of such suggestions is that they may, at times,

    A. be offered primarily for financial reward and not show genuine interest in improvement of work methods
    B. be directed towards making individual jobs easier
    C. be restricted by the employees' fear of radically changing the work methods favored by their supervisors
    D. show little awareness of the effects on the overall objectives and functions of the entire agency

8. Through the supervisory process and relationship, the supervisor is trying to help workers gain increased self-awareness.
   Of the following statements concerning this process, the one which is MOST accurate is:

    A. Self-awareness is developed gradually so that worker can learn to control his own reactions.
    B. Worker is expected to be introspective primarily for his own enlightenment.
    C. Supervisor is trying to help worker handle any emotional difficulties he may reveal.
    D. Worker is expected at the onset to share and determine with the supervisor what in his previous background makes it difficult for him to use certain ideas.

9. The one of the following statements concerning principles in the learning process which is LEAST accurate is:

   A. Some degree of regression on the part of the worker is usually natural in the process of development and this should be accepted by the supervisor.
   B. When a beginning worker shows problems, the supervisor should first handle this behavior as a personality difficulty.
   C. It has been found in the work training process that some degree of resistance is usually inevitable.
   D. The emotional content of work practice may tend to set up *blind spots* in workers.

10. Of the following, the one that represents the BEST basis for planning the content of a successful staff development program is the

    A. time available for meetings
    B. chief social problems of the community
    C. common needs of the staff workers as related to the situations with which they are dealing
    D. experimental programs conducted by other agencies

11. In planning staff development seminars, the MOST valuable topics for discussion are likely to be those selected from

    A. staff suggestions based on the staff's interest and needs
    B. topics recommended for consideration by professional organizations
    C. topics selected by the administration based on demonstrated limitations of staff skill and knowledge
    D. topics selected by the administration based on a combination of staff interest and objectivity evaluated staff needs

12. Staff meetings designed to promote professional staff development are MOST likely to achieve this goal when

    A. there is the widest participation among all staff members who attend the meetings
    B. participation by the most skilled and experienced staff members is predominant
    C. participation by selected staff members is planned before the meeting sessions
    D. supervisory personnel take major responsibility for participation

13. Assume that you are the leader of a conference attended by representatives of various city and private agencies. After the conference has been underway for a considerable time, you realize that the representative of one of these agencies has said nothing. It would generally be BEST for you to

    A. ask him if he would like to say anything
    B. ask the group a pertinent question that he would probably be best able to answer
    C. make no special effort to include him in the conversation
    D. address the next question you planned to ask to him directly

14. A member of a decision-making conference generally makes his BEST contribution to the conference when he

    A. compromises on his own point of view and accepts most of the points of other conference members
    B. persuades the conference to accept all or most of his points

C. persuades the conference to accept his major proposals but will yield on the minor ones
D. succeeds in integrating his ideas with the ideas of the other conference members

15. Of the following, the LEAST accurate statement concerning the compilation and use of statistics in administration is:

    A. Interpretation of statistics is as necessary as their compilation.
    B. Statistical records of expenditures and services are one of the bases for budget preparation.
    C. Statistics on the quality of services rendered to the community will clearly delineate the human values achieved.
    D. The results achieved from collecting and compiling statistics must be in keeping with the cost and effort required.

16. An important administrative problem is how precisely to define the limits on authority that is delegated to subordinate supervisors.
    Such definition of limits of authority SHOULD be

    A. as precise as possible and practicable in all areas
    B. as precise as possible and practicable in all areas of function, but should allow considerable flexibility in the area of personnel management
    C. as precise as possible and practicable in the area of personnel management, but should allow considerable flexibility in the areas of function
    D. in general terms so as to allow considerable flexibility both in the areas of function and in the areas of personnel management

17. The LEAST important of the following reasons why a particular activity should be assigned to a unit which performs activities dissimilar to it is that

    A. close coordination is needed between the particular activity and other activities performed by the unit
    B. it will enhance the reputation and prestige of the unit supervisor
    C. the unit makes frequent use of the results of this particular activity
    D. the unit supervisor has a sound knowledge and understanding of the particular activity

18. The MOST important of the following reasons why the average resident of a deteriorated slum neighborhood resists relocation to an area in the suburbs with better physical accommodations is that he

    A. does not recognize as undesirable the characteristics which are responsible for deterioration of the neighborhood
    B. has some expectation of neighborly assistance in his old home in times of stress and adversity
    C. hopes for better days when he may be able to become a figure of some importance and envy in the old neighborhood
    D. is attuned to the noise of the city and fears the quiet of the suburb

19. From a psychological and sociological point of view, the MOST important of the following dangers to the persons living in an economically depressed area in which the only step taken by governmental and private social agencies to assist these persons is the granting of a dole is that

   A. industry will be reluctant to expand its operations in that area
   B. the dole will encourage additional non-producers to enter the area
   C. the residents of the area will probably have to find their own solution to their problems
   D. their permanent dependency will be fostered

20. The term *real wages* is GENERALLY used by economists to mean the

   A. amount of take-home pay left after taxes, social security, and other such deductions have been made by the employer
   B. average wage actually earned during a calendar or fiscal year
   C. family income expressed on a per capita basis
   D. wages expressed in terms of its buyer power

21. It has, at times, been suggested that an effective way to eradicate juvenile delinquency would be to arrest and punish the parents for the criminal actions of their delinquent children.
    The one of the following which is the CHIEF defect of this proposal is that

   A. it fails to get at the cause of the delinquent act and tends to further weaken disturbed parent-child relationships
   B. since the criminally inclined child has apparently demonstrated little love or affection for his parent, the child will be unlikely to amend his behavior in order to avoid hurting his parent
   C. the child who commits anti-social acts does so in many cases in order to hurt his parents so that this proposal would not only increase the parents' sorrow, but would also serve as an incentive to more delinquency by the child
   D. the punishment should be limited to the person who commits the illegal action rather than to those who are most interested in his welfare

22. Surveys which have compared the relative stability of marriages between white persons with marriages between non-white persons in this country have shown that, among Blacks, there is

   A. a significantly higher percentage of spouses absent from the household than among whites
   B. a significantly higher percentage of spouses absent from the household than among whites living in the South, but the opposite is true in the Northeast
   C. a significantly lower percentage of spouses absent from the household than among whites
   D. no significant difference in the percentage of spouses absent from the household when compared with the white population

23. A phenomenon found in the cultural and recreational patterns of European immigrant families in America is that, generally, the foreign-born adults

    A. as well as their children, tend soon to forget their old-world activities and adopt the cultural and recreational customs of America
    B. as well as their children, tend to retain and continue their old-world cultural and recreational pursuits, and find it equally difficult to adopt those of America
    C. tend soon to drop their old pursuits and adopt the cultural and recreational patterns of America while their children find it somewhat more difficult to make this change
    D. tend to retain and continue their old-world cultural and recreational pursuits while their children tend to rapidly replace these by the games and cultural patterns of America

24. Certain mores of migrant groups are strengthened under the impact of their contact with the native society while other mores are weakened.
    In the case of Puerto Ricans who have come to the city, the effect of such contact upon their traditional family structure has been a

    A. strengthening of the former maternalistic family structure
    B. strengthening of the former paternalistic family structure
    C. weakening of the former maternalistic family structure
    D. weakening of the former paternalistic family structure

25. Administrative reviews and special studies of independent experts, as reported by the Department of Health, Education and Welfare, indicate that the proportion of recipients of public assistance who receive such assistance through *wilful misrepresentation* of the facts is

    A. less than 1%   B. about 4%
    C. between 4% and 7%   D. between 7% and 10%

KEY (CORRECT ANSWERS)

1. B		11. D	
2. D		12. A	
3. D		13. B	
4. B		14. D	
5. A		15. C	
6. B		16. A	
7. D		17. B	
8. A		18. B	
9. B		19. D	
10. C		20. D	

21. A
22. A
23. D
24. D
25. A

TEST 2

DIRECTIONS: Each question or incomplete statement is followed by several suggested answers or completions. Select the one that BEST answers the question or completes the statement. *PRINT THE LETTER OF THE CORRECT ANSWER IN THE SPACE AT THE RIGHT.*

1. In order to meet more adequately the public assistance needs occasioned by sudden changes in the national economy, social service agencies, in general, recommend, as a matter of preference, that

    A. each locality build up reserve funds to care for needy unemployed persons in order to avoid a breakdown of local resources such as occurred during the depression
    B. the federal government assume total responsibility for the administration of public assistance
    C. state settlement laws be strictly enforced so that unemployed workers will be encouraged to move from the emergency industry centers to their former homes
    D. a federal-state-local program of general assistance be established with need as the only eligibility requirement
    E. eligibility requirements be tightened to assure that only legitimately worthy local residents receive the available assistance

    1.____

2. The MOST practical method of maintaining income for the majority of aged persons who are no longer able to work, or for the families of those workers who are deceased, is a(n)

    A. comprehensive system of non-categorical assistance on a basis of cash payments
    B. integrated system of public assistance and extensive work relief programs
    C. co-ordinated system of providing care in institutions and foster homes
    D. system of contributory insurance in which a cash benefit is paid as a matter of right
    E. expanded system of diagnostic and treatment centers

    2.____

3. With the establishment of insurance and assistance programs under the Social Security Act, many institutional programs for the aged have tended to the greatest extent toward an increased emphasis on providing, of the following types of assistance,

    A. care for the aged by denominational groups
    B. care for children requiring institutional treatment
    C. recreational facilities for the able-bodied aged
    D. training facilities in industrial homework for the aged
    E. care for the chronically ill and infirm aged

    3.____

4. Of the following terms, the one which BEST describes the Social Security Act is

    A. enabling legislation
    B. regulatory statute
    C. appropriations act
    D. act of mandamus
    E. provisional enactment

    4.____

5. Of the following, the term which MOST accurately describes an appropriation is

    A. authority to spend
    B. itemized estimate
    C. *fund* accounting
    D. anticipated expenditure
    E. executive budget

6. When business expansion causes a demand for labor, the worker group which benefits MOST immediately is the group comprising

    A. employed workers
    B. inexperienced workers under 21 years of age
    C. experienced workers 21 to 25 years of age
    D. inexperienced older workers
    E. experienced workers over 40 years of age

7. The MOST important failure in our present system of providing social work services in local communities is the

    A. absence of adequate facilities for treating mental illness
    B. lack of coordination of available data and service in the community
    C. poor quality of the casework services provided by the public agencies
    D. limitations of the probation and parole services
    E. inadequacy of private family welfare services

8. Recent studies of the relationship between incidence of illness and the use of available treatment services among various population groups in the United States show that

    A. while lower-income families use medical services with greater frequency, total expenditures are greater among the upper-income groups
    B. although the average duration of a period of medical care increases with increasing income, the average frequency of obtaining care decreases with increasing income
    C. adequacy of medical service is inversely related to frequency of illness and size of family income
    D. families in the higher-income brackets have a heavier incidence of illness and make greater use of medical services than do those in the lower-income brackets
    E. both as to frequency and duration, the distribution of illness falls equally on all groups, but the use of medical services increases with income

9. The category of disease which most public health departments and authorities usually are NOT equipped to handle *directly* is that of

    A. chronic disease
    B. bronchial disturbances
    C. venereal disease
    D. mosquito-borne diseases
    E. incipient forms of tuberculosis

10. Recent statistical analyses of the causes of death in the United States indicate that medical science has now reached the stage where it would be preferable to increase its research toward control, among the following, PRINCIPALLY of

   A. accidents
   B. suicides
   C. communicable disease
   D. chronic disease
   E. infant mortality

11. Although the distinction between mental disease and mental deficiency is fairly definite, both these conditions USUALLY represent

   A. diseases of one part or organ of the body rather than of the whole person
   B. an inadequacy existing from birth or shortly afterwards and appearing as a simplicity of intelligence
   C. a deficiency developing later in life and characterized by distortions of attitude and belief
   D. inadequacies in meeting life situations and in conducting one's affairs
   E. somewhat transitory conditions characterized by disturbances of consciousness

12. According to studies made by reliable medical research organizations in the United States, differences among the states in proportion of physicians to population are MOST directly related to the

   A. geographic resources among the states
   B. skill of the physicians
   C. relative proportions of urban and rural people in the population of the states
   D. number of specialists in the ranks of the physicians
   E. health status of the people in the various states

13. One of the MAIN advantages of incorporating a charitable organization is that

   A. gifts or property of a corporation cannot be held in perpetuity
   B. gifts to unincorporated charitable organizations are not deductible from the taxable income
   C. incorporation gives less legal standing or *personality* than an informal partnership
   D. members of a corporation cannot be held liable for debts contracted by the organization
   E. a corporate organization cannot be sued

14. The BASIC principle underlying a social security program is that the government should provide

   A. aid to families that is not dependent on state or local participation
   B. assistance to any worthy family unable to maintain itself independently
   C. protection to individuals against some of the social risks that are inherent in an industrialized society
   D. safeguards against those factors leading to economic depression

15. The activities of state and local public welfare agencies are dependent to a large degree on the public assistance program of the federal government.
The one of the following which the federal government has NOT been successful in achieving within the local agencies is the

    A. broadening of the scope of public assistance administration
    B. expansion of the categorical programs
    C. improvement of the quality of service given to clients
    D. standardization of the administration of general assistance programs

16. Of the following statements, the one which BEST describes the federal government's position, as stated in the Social Security Act, with regard to tests of character or fitness to be administered by local or state welfare departments to prospective clients is that

    A. no tests of character are required but they are not specifically prohibited
    B. if tests of character are used, they must be uniform throughout the state
    C. tests of character are contrary to the philosophy of the federal government and are to be considered illegal
    D. no tests of character are required, and assistance to those states that use them will be withheld

17. An increase in the size of the welfare grant may increase the cost of the welfare program not only in terms of those already on the welfare rolls, but because it may result in an increase in the number of people on the rolls.
The CHIEF reason that an increase in the size of the grant may cause an increase in the number of people on the rolls is that the increased grant may

    A. induce low-salaried wage earners to apply for assistance rather than continue at their menial jobs
    B. make eligible for assistance many people whose resources are just above the previous standard
    C. induce many people to apply for assistance who hesitated to do so because of meagerness of the previous grant
    D. make relatives less willing to contribute because the welfare grant can more adequately cover their dependents' needs

18. One of the MAIN differences between the use of casework methods by a public welfare agency and by a private welfare agency is that the public welfare agency

    A. requires that the applicant be eligible for the services it offers
    B. cannot maintain a non-judgmental attitude toward its clients because of legal requirements
    C. places less emphasis on efforts to change the behavior of its clients
    D. must be more objective in its approach to the client because public funds are involved

19. All definitions of social casework include certain major assumptions.
Of the following, the one which is NOT considered a major assumption is that

    A. the individual and society are interdependent
    B. social forces influence behavior and attitudes, affording opportunity for self-development and contribution to the world in which we live
    C. reconstruction of the total personality and reorganization of the total environment are specific goals
    D. the client is a responsible participant at every step in the solution of his problems

20. In order to provide those services to problem families which will help restore them to a self-maintaining status, it is necessary to FIRST

    A. develop specific plans to meet the individual needs of the problem family
    B. reduce the size of those caseloads composed of multi-problem families
    C. remove them from their environment and provide them with the means of overcoming their dependency
    D. identify the factors causing their dependency and creating problems for them

21. Of the following, the type of service which can provide the client with the MOST enduring help is that service which

    A. provides him with material aid and relieves the stress of his personal problems
    B. assists him to do as much as he can for himself and leaves him free to make his own decisions
    C. directs his efforts towards returning to a self-maintaining status and provides him with desirable goals
    D. gives him the feeling that the agency is interested in him as an individual and stands ready to assist him with his problems

22. Psychiatric interpretation of unconscious motivations can bring childhood conflicts into the framework of adult understanding and open the way for them to be resolved, but the interpretation must come from within the client.
    This statement means MOST NEARLY that

    A. treatment is merely diagnosis in reverse
    B. explaining a client to himself will lead to the resolution of his problems
    C. the client must arrive at an understanding of his problems
    D. unresolved childhood conflicts create problems for the adult

23. A significant factor in the United States economic picture is the state of the labor market. Of the following, the MOST important development affecting the labor market has been

    A. an expansion of the national defense effort creating new plant capacity
    B. the general increase in personal income as a result of an increase in overtime pay in manufacturing industries
    C. the growth of manufacturing as a result of automation
    D. a demand for a large number of jobs resulting from new job applicants as well as from displacement of workers by automation

24. A typical characteristic of the United States population over 65 is that MOST of them

    A. are independent and capable of self-support
    B. live in their own homes but require various supportive services
    C. live in institutions for the aged
    D. require constant medical attention at home or in an institution

25. The one of the following factors which is MOST important in preventing persons 65 years of age and older from getting employment is the

    A. misconceptions by employers of skills and abilities of senior citizens
    B. lack of skill in modern industrial techniques of persons in this age group
    C. social security laws restricting employment of persons in this age group
    D. unwillingness of persons in this age group to continue supporting themselves

KEY (CORRECT ANSWERS)

1.	D	11.	D
2.	D	12.	C
3.	E	13.	D
4.	A	14.	C
5.	A	15.	D
6.	B	16.	A
7.	B	17.	B
8.	C	18.	C
9.	A	19.	C
10.	D	20.	D

21. B
22. C
23. D
24. B
25. A

EXAMINATION SECTION
TEST 1

DIRECTIONS: Each question or incomplete statement is followed by several suggested answers or completions. Select the one that BEST answers the question or completes the statement. *PRINT THE LETTER OF THE CORRECT ANSWER IN THE SPACE AT THE RIGHT.*

1. An addict who uses the same amount of narcotics each day over a period of time is said to be

    A. systemized
    B. protracted
    C. stabilized
    D. temporized

2. The final phase of the addiction rehabilitation process is USUALLY known as

    A. spin off
    B. re-entry
    C. out straight
    D. wake up

3. If a drug addict says that he *scored*, he MOST likely means that he

    A. bribed a policeman
    B. obtained and used drugs
    C. was detoxified
    D. was arrested and beaten

4. The *synthesis* of a drug refers to its

    A. action
    B. composition
    C. cost
    D. popularity

5. An addict's feeling of well-being from taking drugs is known as feeling

    A. satch
    B. skagg
    C. straight
    D. strung out

6. An addict who is *boosting* is MOST likely engaged in

    A. informing
    B. overdosing
    C. quarreling
    D. stealing

7. A mixture of horse and high C is known as a

    A. flip out
    B. panic
    C. rainbow
    D. speedball

8. *Acapulco gold* is a type of

    A. heroin
    B. marijuana
    C. cocaine
    D. milk sugar

9. *Lebanese Blond* and *Moroccan Black* are slang terms for types of

    A. cocaine
    B. hashish
    C. morphine
    D. peyote

10. The presence of quinine in urine is MOST likely to reveal the use of

    A. glue
    B. hashish
    C. heroin
    D. LSD

11. The percentage of heroin addicts being treated by all existing addiction treatment programs is generally believed to be MOST NEARLY

    A. 5%
    B. 15%
    C. 25%
    D. 35%

12. The BASIC purpose of a referral unit for drug addiction programs is to direct the addict to a treatment program which

    A. applies a conventional form of treatment
    B. employs former addicts in its program
    C. meets his needs in terms of his personality
    D. will adjust him to its program

13. The MAJOR purpose of therapeutic communities is to

    A. change a resident's drug-related behavior, but not his attitudes
    B. enforce outward conformity to acceptable behavior
    C. resocialize a resident to a better lifestyle
    D. get people jobs in the outside world

14. The AVERAGE length of stay for a resident in a therapeutic community is

    A. less than one year
    B. 12 to 18 months
    C. two years
    D. two to three years

15. The one of the following which would MOST quickly increase tension in a therapeutic community is to

    A. prevent new residents from getting mail
    B. stop visits from neighbors
    C. allow new residents to talk with one another
    D. ban coffee and cigarettes

16. MOST persons who have been graduated from therapeutic communities are, in effect, trained for employment in

    A. drug-free programs
    B. youth work agencies
    C. social work agencies
    D. methadone programs

17. In a therapeutic community, the job of knowing everything that is taking place in the facility, particularly the attitudes of individuals, is assigned to the

    A. dingbat
    B. assistant director
    C. expeditor
    D. re-entry leader

18. The Daytop orientation places MAJOR emphasis on

    A. intensive psychoanalysis
    B. the addict's self-responsibility
    C. *polite* forms of group therapy
    D. meditation and isolation

19. Synanon, the California-based therapeutic community, has sought to recruit addicts in New York City for residency in its California facility. The requirements stated by Synanon's local representative are that an applicant must

    A. have a multiple addiction and have failed in a similar program
    B. be over 25 years of age and not be on probation or parole
    C. pay his own plane fare to California and have a sincere desire to *kick* drugs
    D. submit to short-term detoxification and have a stable personality

20. Studies of drug addiction suggest that people are introduced to drugs PRIMARILY through

    A. the activities of drug wholesalers
    B. the seeking after drugs by people for the purpose of experimentation
    C. intimate association with addicts
    D. accidental circumstances

21. When administered in regulated doses, methadone produces

    A. a desire to give up drugs
    B. an anti-alcohol reaction
    C. a stabilized *blockade* phenomenon
    D. changes in basic personality structure

22. In the field of drug addiction treatment, the MAJOR purpose of an induction center is to

    A. provide short-term therapy mainly for *soft* drug abusers
    B. motivate heroin addicts toward long-term treatment
    C. provide a non-threatening residential setting for those who are unwilling to enter a hospital
    D. provide out-patient treatment through chemotherapy

23. Methadone is used in the detoxification of ambulatory heroin users PRIMARILY to

    A. serve as a long-range substitute for heroin
    B. ease the pain of withdrawal
    C. make other therapy unnecessary
    D. overcome multiple addiction

24. Detoxification units usually attempt to do all of the following EXCEPT to

    A. deal with the underlying causes of addiction
    B. direct the patient to an appropriate program after detoxification
    C. free the heroin addict of his physiological habit
    D. administer short-term doses of an opiate antagonist

25. The Food and Drug Administration's proposed regulations on methadone are PRIMARILY intended to

    A. end its diversion for illicit use
    B. ease take-home rules in clinics
    C. make it easier for private doctors to treat addicts
    D. discontinue liquid dosages in clinics

KEY (CORRECT ANSWERS)

1.	C	11.	A
2.	B	12.	C
3.	B	13.	C
4.	B	14.	B
5.	C	15.	D
6.	D	16.	A
7.	D	17.	C
8.	B	18.	B
9.	B	19.	C
10.	C	20.	C

21. C
22. B
23. B
24. A
25. A

TEST 2

DIRECTIONS: Each question or incomplete statement is followed by several suggested answers or completions. Select the one that BEST answers the question or completes the statement. *PRINT THE LETTER OF THE CORRECT ANSWER IN THE SPACE AT THE RIGHT.*

1. One proposal that has been suggested to eliminate the profit motive from the sale of heroin is that drugs be distributed free of charge. However, according to its critics, a MAJOR risk in this approach is that

    A. the total number of addicts may increase
    B. some physicians may become illicit drug sellers
    C. public opinion may cause complete legalization
    D. the potency may be too low for most addicts

    1._____

2. The increase in drug abuse has brought with it an increase in infectious diseases caused by contaminated needles and syringes used for drug injections. Aside from AIDS, one other such disease often fatal is bacterial or fungal endocarditis, which affects the

    A. brain   B. lungs   C. heart   D. liver

    2._____

3. Which of the following is PRIMARILY a chemotherapy technique?

    A. Ambulatory detoxification
    B. Community outreach
    C. Methadone maintenance
    D. Multi-modal therapy

    3._____

4. The mental state brought about by the use of LSD by a normal person is MOST similar to that experienced by

    A. hysterics   B. neurotics
    C. the feeble-minded   D. schizophrenics

    4._____

5. The one of the following statements which is accurate according to a study sponsored by the National Commission on Marijuana and Drug Abuse is that heavy use of marijuana

    A. impairs performance on tests of cognitive or motor function
    B. does not interfere with the perception of the rate at which time passes
    C. improves the ability to recall recent events
    D. does not decrease the motivation to work

    5._____

6. The MOST serious withdrawal symptoms are USUALLY produced by the discontinuance of

    A. barbiturates   B. cocaine
    C. heroin   D. *ice*

    6._____

7. A characteristic of a methedrine user who regularly injects the drug directly into his bloodstream is that he

    A. becomes addicted
    B. usually becomes depressed during his *high*
    C. often exhausts his mental and physical reserves
    D. seldom becomes violent

    7._____

8. The initial observable effects following glue-sniffing are MOST likely to be

   A. loss of memory, headaches, and slowness in response
   B. spasms of the muscles of the neck and the lower extremities
   C. sneezing, coughing, and drooling
   D. similar to drunken behavior and a vague joyousness of manner

9. As the user's dosage of a psychoactive agent is increased, his response is MOST likely to be influenced by factors which are

   A. environmental
   B. pharmacological
   C. psychological
   D. social

10. In the treatment of heroin addicts, the use of cyclazocine is considered by some medical experts to be preferable to methadone PRIMARILY because, in general, the use of cyclazocine

    A. cuts the cost of treatment by approximately 40%, compared to the use of methadone
    B. does not produce the allergic side effects sometimes associated with methadone
    C. shortens the period of time necessary for treatment
    D. significantly reduces the need for auxiliary supportive services

11. The mixture which addicts inject into their companions who have taken an overdose of heroin is composed of

    A. sugar and coffee
    B. nutmeg and alcohol
    C. salt and water
    D. sugar and peroxide

12. MOST of the estimated 300,000 alcoholics residing in the city are

    A. employed
    B. skid row types
    C. under treatment
    D. under 27 years of age

13. Employee alcoholism programs are usually more effective than community programs MAINLY because

    A. most alcoholics are more cooperative in a friendly setting
    B. continued employment usually depends upon a successful recovery
    C. employers spend more funds for their programs because of the high standards set by the Industrial Conference Board
    D. penalties generally imposed against employers for alcohol-precipitated accidents are severe

14. Which of the following is an addiction treatment program operated DIRECTLY by the Addiction Services Agency?

    A. Addicts Rehabilitation Center
    B. Horizon Project
    C. Odyssey House
    D. Reality House

15. The Vera Institute's Heroin Treatment Plan is PRIMARILY intended to reach those who 15.____

    A. acquired a serious addiction in the U.S. Armed Forces
    B. are over age 35 and have used heroin for 15 years
    C. have failed on methadone and refuse treatment not involving heroin
    D. have been convicted of a drug-related felony

16. The State Narcotics Addiction Control Commission is PRIMARILY concerned with treating 16.____

    A. addicted war veterans
    B. criminal addicts
    C. youthful drug experimenters
    D. non-opiate substance abusers

17. Under the State Youthful Drug Abuser Act, a number of programs are conducted in the schools. The basic principle upon which all of these programs are founded is that drug addiction is GENERALLY attributed to 17.____

    A. frustration with school
    B. individual pathology
    C. adult group pressures
    D. political and environmental forces

18. Out-patient units using the youth center approach USUALLY concentrate on young people who 18.____

    A. are at a low level of drug abuse
    B. are likely to become habitual users of marijuana
    C. experiment with substances that are not considered dangerous
    D. are addicted to the use of common hard drugs

19. In order to determine the degree to which participants in youth-oriented addiction programs successfully manage to pursue positive life goals, *before* and *after* studies should be made of all such participants. Which of the following would be the LEAST useful measure in such studies? 19.____

    A. School attendance
    B. Non-delinquent behavior
    C. Salary earned after treatment
    D. Withdrawal from the drug culture

20. Those who conduct drug education programs in the urban school setting USUALLY find that younger children are 20.____

    A. particularly knowledgeable about the costs of drugs
    B. indifferent to drug education as currently presented
    C. highly motivated to learn about drug abuse
    D. mainly interested in the history of drug traffic

21. Federal law enforcement officials sometimes ignore street addicts and general drug abusers mainly because the MAJOR concern of federal officials in fighting drug abuse is to

    A. concentrate on interstate criminal activities since they are federal offenses
    B. encourage local officials to develop appropriate law enforcement capabilities
    C. gather information for technical studies and schedules of controlled substances
    D. stop organized drug traffic by prosecuting high-level importers, dealers, and distributors

22. The Narcotics Register is maintained by the

    A. Addiction Services Agency
    B. Bureau of Mental Health
    C. Department of Health
    D. Health and Hospitals Corporation

23. In a recent poll, it was found that, compared to the sixties, college students today

    A. confine their use of drugs and other substances to a small circle of friends
    B. have almost entirely abandoned substance abuse in favor of various religious and mystical practices
    C. use amphetamines about as often as they use alcohol
    D. were more likely to use marijuana and cocaine

24. Crimes committed by drug addicts MOST often victimize the

    A. middle class in outlying sections
    B. poor in slum areas
    C. wealthy in exclusive sections
    D. foreign-born in ethnic enclaves

25. The National Commission on Marijuana and Drug Abuse unanimously recommended, with regard to marijuana,

    A. eliminating all criminal penalties for its private use and possession
    B. increasing civil penalties for anti-social acts committed under its influence
    C. classifying its use by adults as a misdemeanor
    D. encouraging its use as a substitute for alcohol

KEY (CORRECT ANSWERS)

1.	A	11.	C
2.	C	12.	A
3.	C	13.	B
4.	D	14.	B
5.	A	15.	C
6.	A	16.	B
7.	C	17.	B
8.	D	18.	A
9.	B	19.	C
10.	C	20.	C

21. D
22. C
23. D
24. B
25. A

TEST 3

DIRECTIONS: Each question or incomplete statement is followed by several suggested answers or completions. Select the one that BEST answers the question or completes the statement. *PRINT THE LETTER OF THE CORRECT ANSWER IN THE SPACE AT THE RIGHT.*

Questions 1-3.

DIRECTIONS: Questions 1 through 3 are to be answered SOLELY on the basis of the following paragraph.

A substantial source of opposition to legalising heroin is those people who are convinced that this idea is simply another form of social and economic injustice. Instead of getting at the fundamental causes of addiction, they say, the result will be to turn hundreds of young addicts into the living dead.

1. According to the above paragraph, opposition to legalizing heroin is based, in part, on the belief that

    A. some addicts will become walking dead people
    B. the problem is entirely one of educating individuals
    C. the pushers will simply turn to other criminal activities
    D. the root causes of addiction are still mysterious

2. Which of the following treatment approaches would the author of the above paragraph be MOST likely to oppose?

    A. Ambulatory detoxification
    B. Methadone maintenance
    C. Drug-free therapeutic community
    D. Youth intervention program

3. As used in the paragraph, the underlined word *substantial* means MOST NEARLY

    A. known   B. large   C. strange   D. unanimous

Questions 4-8.

DIRECTIONS: Questions 4 through 8 are to be answered SOLELY on the basis of the following paragraph.

In the past dozen years or so, there has emerged an argument which obviously has a certain persuasiveness among young people: that drugs are being used not as an expression of antisocial behavior or for escape, but to define a different, anti-establishment culture. Drugs can, of course, be used that way; it's very possible to have a youth culture that uses drugs as a norm. But it's also possible to have a youth culture that is opposed to using drugs as a norm. For example, in China, around 1910, a very effective campaign against opium was led largely by students who felt that the use of drugs was the reason China had suffered so much at the hands of the Western powers.

4. According to the above paragraph, the Chinese students opposed the use of opium because

   A. it contradicted Chinese religious values
   B. it interfered with their studies
   C. they believed it weakened their country
   D. the Western powers encouraged addiction

5. The writer of the above paragraph seems to believe that there is no necessary connection between

   A. escapism and culture
   B. norms and values
   C. students and politics
   D. youth and drugs

6. According to the above paragraph, it is possible to have a youth culture that considers the use of drugs

   A. completely acceptable
   B. legally defensible
   C. morally uplifting
   D. physically beneficial

7. The underlined word *emerged* means MOST NEARLY

   A. come into view
   B. gone through
   C. required to be
   D. responded quickly

8. As used in the above paragraph, the underlined word *norm* means MOST NEARLY

   A. argument or explanation
   B. error or mistake
   C. pleasure or reward
   D. rule or average

Questions 9-11.

DIRECTIONS: Questions 9 through 11 are to be answered SOLELY on the basis of the following paragraph.

Drug abuse prevention efforts are only in their beginning stages. Far less is known about how to design programs that successfully counter the seductive effects which drugs have upon the young than about how to build clinics and programs to treat those who have become addicts. The latter can be done with enough dollars, managerial competence, and qualified personnel. The former depends upon such intangibles as community leadership, personal attitudes, and, in the final analysis, individual choices. Given this void in our society's understanding of what it is that makes us so vulnerable to addiction, government must build upon its growing experience to invest wisely in those efforts that offer positive alternatives to drug abuse.

9. The one of the following which is probably the BEST title for the above paragraph is

   A. The Youthful Drug Abuser
   B. Government's Management of Drug Programs
   C. A Scientific Analysis of Drug Cures
   D. The Difficulty of Drug Abuse Prevention

10. According to the above paragraph, treating drug addicts, as compared to preventing drug addiction among the young, is GENERALLY

    A. *easier,* mainly because there is more public interest in this method
    B. *harder,* mainly because qualified personnel are not readily available
    C. *easier,* mainly because there is more known about how to accomplish this objective
    D. *harder,* mainly because confirmed drug addicts do not give up the habit readily

11. According to the above paragraph, the role of government in dealing with the problem of drug addiction and youth should be to

    A. build larger clinics and develop additional programs for treatment of offenders
    B. help attract youth to behavior which is more desirable than that provided by the drug culture
    C. provide the funds and personnel essential to successful enforcement programs
    D. establish centers for the study and analysis of those factors that make our citizens vulnerable to addiction

Questions 12-15.

DIRECTIONS: Questions 12 through 15 are to be answered SOLELY on the basis of the following paragraph.

Alcoholics are to be found in both sexes, in every major religious and racial group, and at all socio-economic levels. What they share in common are psychiatric problems which they seek to ease or dull through alcohol. Ideally, every heavy drinker should be subjected to <u>intensive</u> psychiatric therapy. Unfortunately, even psychiatric treatment is not always successful, and in any case the nation has <u>allocated</u> neither the funds nor the personnel nor the facilities that would be required for such a massive therapeutic effort.

12. According to the above paragraph, national priorities in connection with psychiatric treatment for alcoholism do NOT provide for

    A. fair and impartial treatment
    B. large-scale programs
    C. proper religious values
    D. strict laws against alcoholism

13. According to the above paragraph, alcoholics are MOST likely to be

    A. emotionally disturbed   B. ultimately curable
    C. unable to function   D. under medical care

14. As used in the above paragraph, the underlined word *intensive* means MOST NEARLY

    A. concentrated   B. modern
    C. prompt   D. specialized

15. As used in the above paragraph, the underlined word *allocated* means MOST NEARLY

    A. assigned   B. conserved   C. desired   D. recognized

KEY (CORRECT ANSWERS)

1. A
2. B
3. B
4. C
5. D

6. A
7. A
8. D
9. D
10. C

11. B
12. B
13. A
14. A
15. A

EXAMINATION SECTION
TEST 1

DIRECTIONS: Each question or incomplete statement is followed by several suggested answers or completions. Select the one that BEST answers the question or completes the statement. *PRINT THE LETTER OF THE CORRECT ANSWER IN THE SPACE AT THE RIGHT.*

1. Making an illegal purchase of drugs is known as

    A. popping   B. rushing   C. scagging   D. scoring

2. A narcotics detective is known as a

    A. narc   B. red bull   C. mule   D. schmeck

3. *Speed* is a street term for an often-abused drug which is sometimes used in the treatment of

    A. allergies   B. epilepsy   C. insomnia   D. obesity

4. An addict who is *copping* would MOST likely be

    A. attempting detoxification
    B. engaged in crime
    C. undergoing therapy
    D. under emotional stress

5. An inert or neutral substance given to a person who requests unneeded medication, or used in an experiment where it is necessary to secretly substitute an inactive substance for an active substance, is known as a

    A. cross-over   B. placebo
    C. response   D. sedative

6. The *generic* name of a drug is the name that is

    A. a popular street term in general usage
    B. an abbreviation of the hospital name
    C. chemically, pharmacologically, or technically descriptive
    D. used as a trademark by its manufacturer

7. The physiological effect that the abuse of a specific substance will have on an individual person is LEAST likely to be influenced by the substance's

    A. dosage   B. frequency of use
    C. potency   D. street cost

8. Two kinds of patients in need of detoxification are heroin addicts and serious abusers of

    A. barbiturates   B. cocaine
    C. volatile substances   D. mescaline

9. An amphetamine abuser's prolonged sleep, lasting a day or two, is known as

    A. bugging   B. flaking   C. crashing   D. zonking

10. Chemical solvents are substances subject to abuse USUALLY by means of

   A. ingestion
   B. inhalation
   C. subcutaneous injection
   D. skin absorption

11. Of the following, it is LEAST desirable for a drug-free day care center to

   A. be situated in a low drug abuse area
   B. have kitchen facilities on the premises
   C. be located near public transportation
   D. provide treatment on weekends

12. Of the following, the MAIN justification for minimal security measures at a drug-free day care center is that

   A. the people on the premises are trustworthy
   B. the clients might otherwise be insulted
   C. there are no unauthorized visitors on the premises
   D. there are no drugs on the premises

13. No applicant may be processed for admission to a methadone treatment program unless it has been verified that he meets all Federal criteria for admission and

   A. an exact dosage has been determined and prescribed for him by the attending physician for daily administration in liquid form
   B. the applicant properly signs a waiver giving his informal consent to forego drug-free types of treatment
   C. the methadone treatment program is not serving more than 150 rehabilitants at any one time
   D. the sources and methods of such verification have been recorded as specific documentation in the applicant's case folder

14. The following statements refer to abuse of amphetamine:
   I. Contrary to popular belief, amphetamine abuse rarely kills
   II. Long-term high-dose intravenous injection of amphetamine will usually induce paranoid psychosis symptoms
   III. Sleep deprivation worsens and complicates the direct pharmacological effects of amphetamine

   Which of the following choices lists all of the above statements that are CORRECT?

   A. I *only*
   B. I and III *only*
   C. II and III *only*
   D. I, II, and III

15. In a methadone treatment program, unless another method has been approved, urine specimens must be collected

   A. *before* the patient has eaten breakfast
   B. *in* containers which are provided in sterile condition
   C. *under* the visual supervision of a staff member
   D. *within* one hour after the patient has eaten breakfast

16. In a methadone treatment program, urine specimens must be acquired in accordance with a randomized schedule. A schedule which is *randomized* provides for specimens to be collected from individual patients

    A. carefully
    B. intensely
    C. irregularly
    D. privately

17. In a methadone treatment program, a problem patient should be removed from the program if his misbehavior results from

    A. a temporary phase he is undergoing
    B. violent acting-out
    C. deterioration of personality
    D. pathological depression

18. According to the outpatient drug-free treatment manual, card-playing and pool should be de-emphasized in a drug-free day care program PRIMARILY because such activities

    A. appear as unbusinesslike to participants
    B. are usually of little interest to participants
    C. tend to be unfamiliar to participants
    D. relate to and reinforce participants' past negative lifestyle

19. To be selected for participation in the A.S.A. Court Referral Project, an individual must not be charged with certain crimes.
    Which of the following choices does NOT mention a crime that would probably bar participation in this project?

    A. Aggravated assault, embezzlement
    B. Forgery, larceny
    C. Reckless endangerment, armed robbery
    D. Felonious assault, theft of services

20. Federal regulations concerning the confidentiality of the records of drug abuse patients require that such records be disclosed only for certain purposes and under certain circumstances.
    Following are three possible reasons for disclosure:
    I. To medical personnel to the extent necessary to meet a genuine medical emergency
    II. To a qualified academic research person who affirms that his published report will contain only objective statements and only the names of former patients
    III. One authorized by an appropriate order of a court of competent jurisdiction granted after application showing good cause therefor
    Which of the following choices lists all of the above statements that describe PROPER reasons for disclosure?

    A. I and II *only*
    B. II and III *only*
    C. I and III *only*
    D. I, II, and III

21. Opinions vary as to whether caffeine is addicting, depending upon the definition of addiction. However, caffeine is a potent poison when taken in very large doses.
Which of the following over-the-counter preparations contains caffeine in concentrated form?

   A. Compoz   B. NoDoz   C. Nytol   D. Sominex

22. A recent study showed that while many teenagers are convinced that cigarette smoking causes cancer and heart attacks, they still start to smoke cigarettes. One major reason for their starting to smoke, according to the study, is that they have not been told that nicotine is an addicting drug.
The DIRECT result of such lack of knowledge is that most of them who become smokers

   A. start smoking because their elders smoke
   B. imitate other teenagers and begin smoking
   C. lack knowledge of the Surgeon General's findings on the dangers of smoking
   D. expect to stop smoking at some future time

23. Researchers have asked young drug users why they first began to use drugs.
The MOST common answer is

   A. the influence of profit-motivated pushers
   B. peer-group pressures
   C. enjoyment of drug-taking
   D. a family member's example

24. Researchers have found that young drug users who had not sought treatment offered several different explanations for not doing so.
The MOST common reason given was that the individual

   A. believed that he did not need help
   B. never thought about treatment
   C. was discouraged by rumors of waiting lists
   D. was unfamiliar with the types of treatment available

25. Those who have had any success in treating drug addicts are certain of one thing. Without the willing cooperation of the addicts themselves in the treatment leading to a cure, you will get nowhere.
Based on this viewpoint, it is MOST reasonable to state that in order to treat addicts successfully it is necessary for workers to

   A. view the problem of addiction as the addicts themselves do
   B. realize that total drug abstinence is necessary for rehabilitation
   C. first attempt to alter the addict's lifestyle
   D. employ the *up-front* techniques of encounter groups and similar confrontation therapies

KEY (CORRECT ANSWERS)

1. D
2. A
3. D
4. B
5. B

6. C
7. D
8. A
9. C
10. B

11. A
12. D
13. D
14. D
15. C

16. C
17. B
18. D
19. B
20. C

21. B
22. D
23. B
24. A
25. A

TEST 2

DIRECTIONS: Each question or incomplete statement is followed by several suggested answers or completions. Select the one that BEST answers the question or completes the statement. *PRINT THE LETTER OF THE CORRECT ANSWER IN THE SPACE AT THE RIGHT.*

1. In many societies in which use or abuse of a substance has been largely restricted to the lowest social classes, it is often difficult to know to what extent ascribed characteristics of users represent alterations related to such use or the institutionalized prejudices of persons of higher social status.
Based on the foregoing statement *only,* it is MOST reasonable to state that substance abusers in such societies are

   A. indifferent to the legal rights of other people
   B. likely to be members of the least advantaged groups
   C. tradition-bound and therefore unwilling to alter their lifestyle
   D. ignorant of the long-term harmfulness of substance abuse

2. It is not really known whether substance abuse causes a loss of conventional competitive motivation among youth. The one of the following statements which BEST explains this lack of knowledge is:

   A. Drug users are found in all age groups and social classes, not merely among alienated youth
   B. Little evidence exists to support the theory that unmotivated youth could develop and establish a counterculture
   C. It is often difficult to distinguish a possible drug-related loss of motivation from that produced by the prevailing values found among youth
   D. Loss of motivation is the underlying cause of decreasing interest in traditional values, but there is little agreement on a definition of such values

3. The following three statements refer to marijuana use in the United States:
   I. Use is highly age-related and, to a lesser extent, to educational status
   II. Use is more common among rural residents than among urban residents
   III. A daily user is less likely to sell *(deal)* than is a monthly user
   Which of the following choices CORRECTLY classifies the above statements into those which are correct and those which are not?

   A. I is correct, but II and III are not.
   B. I and II are correct, but III is not.
   C. III is correct, but I and II are not.
   D. II and III are correct, but I is not.

4. Clients referred to a methadone program are MOST likely to

   A. be willing to accept strongly interactive therapy
   B. benefit from a highly structured environment
   C. have little potential for self-support through legitimate employment
   D. have the social support of friends or family

5. Professional social workers have at times been criticized, by those who favor the ex-addict leadership mode, for taking erroneous approaches to the treatment of addiction. The MOST common erroneous approach of professional social workers is said to be the tendency to

   A. believe that addicts derive great pleasure in the release from psychic tension that drugs provide
   B. expect an ideal client and an ideal client-worker relationship
   C. give high priority to drugs and their use as the major concern of the abuser's life
   D. sacrifice the role of psychotherapist for one of a strong helping figure

6. Researchers have recommended several changes in drug treatment programs. Which of the following is NOT one of these recommendations?

   A. Sixteen- and seventeen-year-old drug abusers should be given special treatment.
   B. The age requirement for entering methadone maintenance programs should be lowered.
   C. The requirement of parental consent for a minor to enter a drug treatment program should be eliminated.
   D. The use of rehabilitated youthful drug abusers to educate others about the true conditions in treatment programs should be discouraged.

7. Following are three statements which may or may not be correct about drug users:
   I. An insignificant percentage of the drug users had begun their drug use by the age of 11.
   II. Most of the drug users use crack alone.
   III. Most of the drug users are regular users, using drugs at least once a week.

   Which of the following choices CORRECTLY classifies the above statements into those which are correct and those which are not?

   A. I is correct, but II and III are not.
   B. III is correct, but I and II are not.
   C. I and II are correct, but III is not.
   D. II and III are correct, but I is not.

8. Because of the fad-like aspects of marijuana use, it can be expected that rates of use at individual high schools and colleges will _____ the national averages.

   A. *be identical* to
   B. *lag behind*
   C. *remain stable* despite fluctuations in
   D. *vary widely* from

9. In developing staffing requirements for a new drug-free day care center, which of the following is LEAST important?
   The

   A. size of the planned program
   B. treatment philosophy to be followed at the center
   C. ages of potential staff members
   D. availability of ancillary community resources

10. In the recruitment of new staff for a drug-free day care center, emphasis should be placed PRIMARILY on an applicant's having

    A. therapeutic skills
    B. a knowledge of community resources
    C. no history of drug use
    D. the ability to teach vocational rehabilitation

11. In social research, the selection of a good test involves considering a number of criteria. The MOST important single criterion is the test's

    A. popularity   B. format
    C. simplicity   D. validity

12. Of the following substances, the one MOST often and closely associated with homicides and aggressive assaults is

    A. marijuana   B. crack
    C. alcohol   D. barbiturates

13. The phenomenon of _____ has caused an epidemic in drug use. The use of _____, which had declined, is on an upswing. _____ was part of an effective treatment program but the abuses of its administration and the subsequent increase in those addicted to it have rendered its future use in doubt.

    A. ice; marijuana; cocaine
    B. heroin; cocaine; methadone
    C. crack; marijuana; ice
    D. crack; heroin; methadone

14. Which of the following statements BEST characterizes the position of the Administration on marijuana use?

    A. Its illegality is a deterrent to large numbers of potential users.
    B. Its prohibition serves to clutter the courts, diverts the police from attending to serious crimes, and enriches the legal profession.
    C. Public policy regarding its use should be made analogous to current policy regarding alcohol and tobacco.
    D. The central issue stemming from its use is the erosion of the nation's moral fiber, not the narrow question of penalties or stigmatization.

15. A community's opinion about a new addiction treatment center located in the neighborhood is LEAST likely to be favorably affected by

    A. permitting visits by community residents
    B. press releases and advertisements
    C. the behavior and attitude of participants or clients
    D. discussions between the center's director and members of local organizations

16. Assume that you are assigned to give an informal talk, including a question-and-answer session, to a community group in order to tell them about a new program of the addiction services agency.
    In order to carry out this assignment, you should consider doing each of the following EXCEPT

    A. preparing an outline of the speech
    B. beginning the speech with an attention-getting opening
    C. giving standard, memorized answers to questions without deviation
    D. closing the speech with a brief summary

17. Experienced public speakers sometimes attempt to gain rapport with the audience by leading the audience to identify themselves with the speaker or to identify him with something they find admirable. For example, the speaker may remark, *I was born and grew up in this neighborhood,* or *I, like many of you, am married and have children,* or whatever else he thinks will be meaningful to his audience.
    Of the following, which is the GREATEST danger of this approach?
    The

    A. basic feelings and cultural patterns of the audience may be ignored
    B. attempt to deceive the audience is doomed to failure
    C. audience will become interested in the speaker as a person
    D. link between the speaker's life and the audience's life may seem remote

18. Assume that you have planned a general public information program on drug addiction prevention which employs various techniques of presenting information. You have scheduled a presentation at a large community center, which you expect to be well-attended. Shortly before this meeting, several community leaders inform you that many people are interested in a problem which you know is not dealt with in your material. Which of the following materials which you have already prepared could you adapt MOST quickly to meet this changed situation?

    A. Booklet
    B. Film
    C. Speech outline
    D. Slide show with synchronized taped commentary

19. When a public agency conducts a public relations program, it is MOST likely to find that each recipient of its message will

    A. disagree with the basic purpose of the message if the officials are not well known to him
    B. accept the message if it is presented by someone perceived as having a definite intention to persuade
    C. ignore the message unless it is presented in a literate and clever manner
    D. give greater attention to certain portions of the message as a result of his individual and cultural differences

20. Following are three statements about public relations and communications:
    I. A person who seeks to influence public opinion can speed up a trend.
    II. Mass communications is the exposure of a mass audience to an idea.
    III. All media are equally effective in reaching opinion leaders.

    Which of the following choices CORRECTLY classifies the above statements into those which are correct and those which are not?

    A. I and II are correct, but III is not.
    B. II and III are correct, but I is not.
    C. I and III are correct, but II is not.
    D. III is correct, but I and II are not.

20.____

KEY (CORRECT ANSWERS)

1.	B	11.	D
2.	C	12.	C
3.	A	13.	D
4.	D	14.	A
5.	B	15.	B
6.	D	16.	C
7.	B	17.	D
8.	D	18.	C
9.	C	19.	D
10.	A	20.	A

EXAMINATION SECTION
TEST 1

DIRECTIONS: Each question or incomplete statement is followed by several suggested answers or completions. Select the one that BEST answers the question or completes the statement. *PRINT THE LETTER OF THE CORRECT ANSWER IN THE SPACE AT THE RIGHT.*

1. When a counselor is planning a future interview with a client, of the following, the MOST important consideration is the

    A. recommendations he will make to the client
    B. place where the client will be interviewed
    C. purpose for which the client will be interviewed
    D. personality of the client

2. For a counselor to make a practice of reviewing the client's case record, if available, prior to the interview, is, usually,

    A. *inadvisable*, because knowledge of the client's past record will tend to influence the counselor's judgment
    B. *advisable*, because knowledge of the client's background will help the counselor to identify discrepancies in the client's responses
    C. *inadvisable*, because such review is time-consuming and of questionable value
    D. *advisable*, because knowledge of the client's background will help the counselor to understand the client's situation

3. Assume that a counselor makes a practice of constantly reassuring clients with serious and complex problems by making such statements as: "I'm sure you'll soon be well;" "I know you'll get a job soon;" or "Everything will be all right."
Of the following, the MOST likely result of such a practice is to

    A. encourage the client and make him feel that the counselor understands what the client is going through
    B. make the client doubtful about the counselor's understanding of his difficulties and the counselor's ability to help
    C. confuse the client and cause him to hesitate to take any action on his own initiative
    D. help the client to be more realistic about his situation and the probability that it will improve

4. In order to get the maximum amount of information from a client during an interview, of the following, it is MOST important for the counselor to communicate to the client the feeling that the counselor is

    A. interested in the client
    B. a figure of authority
    C. efficient in his work habits
    D. sympathetic to the client's lifestyle

5. Of the following, the counselor who takes extremely detailed notes during an interview with a client is *most likely* to

    A. encourage the client to talk freely

B. distract and antagonize the client
C. help the client feel at ease
D. understand the client's feelings

6. As a counselor, you find that many of the clients you interview are verbally abusive and unusually hostile to you.
   Of the following, the MOST appropriate action for you to take *first* is to

   A. review your interviewing techniques and consider whether you may be provoking these clients
   B. act in a more authoritative manner when interviewing troublesome clients
   C. tell these clients that you will not process their applications unless their troublesome behavior ceases
   D. disregard the clients' troublesome behavior during the interview

7. During an interview, you did not completely understand several of your client's responses. In each instance, you rephrased the client's statement and asked the client if that was what he meant.
   For you to use such a technique during interviews would be considered

   A. *inappropriate;* you may have distorted the client's meaning by rephrasing his statements
   B. *inappropriate;* you should have asked the same questioE until you received a comprehensible response
   C. *appropriate;* the client will have a chance to correct you if you have misinterpreted his responses
   D. *appropriate;* a counselor should rephrase clients' responses for the records

8. A counselor is interviewing a client who has just had a severe emotional shock because of an assault on her by a mugger.
   Of the following, the approach which would generally be MOST helpful to the client is for the counselor to

   A. comfort the client and encourage her to talk about the assault
   B. sympathize with the client but refuse to discuss the assault with her
   C. tell the client to control her emotions and think positively about the future
   D. proceed with the interview in an impersonal and unemotional manner

9. A counselor finds that her questions are misinterpreted by many of the clients she interviews.
   Of the following, the MOST likely reason for this problem is that the

   A. client is not listening attentively
   B. client wants to avoid the subject being discussed
   C. counselor has failed to express her meaning clearly
   D. counselor has failed to put the client at ease

10. For a counselor to look directly at the client and observe him during the interview is generally

    A. *inadvisable;* this will make the client nervous and uncomfortable
    B. *advisable;* the client will be more likely to refrain from lying
    C. *inadvisable;* the counselor will not be able to take notes for the case record
    D. *advisable;* this will encourage conversation and accelerate the progress of the interview

11. You are interviewing a client who is applying for social services for the first time. In order to encourage this client to freely give you the information needed for you to establish his eligibility, of the following, the BEST way to start the interview is by

    A. asking questions the client can easily answer
    B. conveying the impression that his responses to your questions will be checked
    C. asking two or three similar but important questions
    D. assuring the client that your sole responsibility is "getting the facts"

12. Counselors are encouraged to record significant information obtained from clients and services provided for clients. Of the following, the MOST important reason for this practice is that these case records will

    A. help to reduce the need for regular supervisory conferences
    B. indicate to counselors which clients are taking up the most time
    C. provide information which will help the agency to improve its services to clients
    D. make it easier to verify the complaints of clients

13. As a counselor you find that interviews can be completed in a shorter period of time if you ask questions which limit the client to a certain answer.
    For you to use such a technique would be considered

    A. *inappropriate,* because this type of question usually requires advance preparation
    B. *inappropriate,* because this type of question may inhibit the client from saying what he really means
    C. *appropriate,* because you know the areas into which the questions should be directed
    D. *appropriate,* because this type of question usually helps clients to express themselves clearly

14. Assume that, while you are interviewing an individual to obtain information, the individual pauses in the middle of an answer.
    The BEST of the following actions for you to take at this time is to

    A. correct any inaccuracies in what he has said
    B. remain silent until he continues
    C. explain your position on the matter being discussed
    D. explain that time is short and that he must complete his story quickly

15. You have been assigned to interview the mother of a five-year-old son in her home to get information useful in locating the child's absent father. During the interview, you notice many serious bruises on the child's arms and legs, which the mother explains are due to the child's clumsiness. Of the following, your BEST course of action is to

    A. accept the mother's explanation and concentrate on getting information which will help you to locate the father
    B. advise the mother to have the child examined for a medical condition that may be causing his clumsiness
    C. make a surprise visit to the mother later, to see if someone is beating the child
    D. complete your interview with the mother and report the case to your supervisor for investigation of possible child abuse

16. During an interview, the former landlord of an absent father offers to help you to locate the father if you will give the landlord confidential information you have on the financial situation of the father.
    Of the following, you should

    A. immediately end the interview with the landlord
    B. urge the landlord to help you but explain that you are not permitted to give him confidential information
    C. freely give the landlord the confidential information he requests about the father
    D. give the landlord the information only if he promises to keep it confidential

17. You feel that your client, a released mental patient, is not adjusting well to living on his own in an apartment. To gather more information, you interview privately his next-door neighbor, who claims that the client is creating a "disturbance" and speaks of the client in an angry and insulting manner.
    Of the following, the BEST action for you to take in this situation is to

    A. listen patiently to the neighbor to try to get the facts about your client's behavior
    B. inform the neighbor that he has no right to speak insultingly about a mentally ill person
    C. make an appointment to interview the neighbor some other time when he isn't so upset
    D. tell the neighbor that you were not aware of the client's behavior and that you will have the client moved

18. As a counselor, you are interviewing a client to determine his eligibility for a work program. Suddenly the client begins to shout that he is in no condition to work and that you are persecuting him for no reason.
    Of the following, your BEST response to this client is to

    A. advise the client to stop shouting or you will call for the security guard
    B. wait until the client calms down, then order him to come back for another interview
    C. insist that you are not persecuting the client and that he must complete the interview
    D. wait until the client calms down, say that you understand how he feels, and try to continue the interview

19. You are interviewing a mother whose 17-year-old son has recently been returned home from a mental institution. Although she is willing to care for her son at home, she is frightened by his strange and sometimes violent behavior and does not know the best arrangement to make for his care.
    Of the following, your MOST appropriate response to this mother's problem is to

    A. describe the supportive services and alternatives to home care which are available
    B. help her to accept her son's strange and violent behavior
    C. tell her that she will not be permitted to care for her son at home if she is frightened by his behavior
    D. convince her that she is not responsible for her son's mental condition

20. Assume that you are interviewing an elderly man who comes to the center several times a month to discuss topics with you which are not related to social services. You realize that the man is lonely and enjoys these conversations.
    Of the following, it would be MOST appropriate to

    A. politely discourage the man from coming in to pass the time with you
    B. avoid speaking to this man the next time he comes into the center
    C. explore with the client his feelings about joining a senior citizens' center
    D. continue to hold these conversations with the man

21. A client you are interviewing tends to ramble on after each response that he gives, so that many clients are kept waiting.
    In this situation, of the following, it would be MOST advisable to

    A. try to direct the interview, in order to obtain the necessary information
    B. reduce the number of questions asked so that you can shorten the interview
    C. arrange a second interview for the client so that you can give him more time
    D. tell the client that he is wasting everybody's time

22. A non-minority counselor is about to interview a minority client on public assistance for job placement when the client says: "What does your kind know about my problems? You've never had to survive out on these streets."
    Of the following, the counselor's MOST appropriate response in this situation is to

    A. postpone the interview until a minority counselor is available to interview the client
    B. tell the client that he must cooperate with the counselor if he wants to continue receiving public assistance
    C. explain to the client the function of the counselor in this unit and the services he provides
    D. assure the client that you do not have to be a member of a minority group to understand the effects of poverty

23. When you are interviewing someone to obtain information, the BEST of the following reasons for you to repeat certain of his exact words is to

    A. *assure* him that appropriate action will be taken
    B. *encourage* him to elaborate on a point he has made
    C. *assure* him that you agree with his point of view
    D. *encourage* him to switch to another topic of discussion

24. fou are interviewing a young client who seriously under-estimates the amount of education and training he will require for a certain occupation.
    For you to tell the client that you think he is mistaken would generally be considered

    A. *inadvisable*, because counselors should not express their opinions to clients
    B. *inadvisable*, because clients have the right to self-determination
    C. *advisable*, because clients should generally be alerted to their misconceptions
    D. *advisable*, because counselors should convince clients to adopt a proper life style

25. Of the following, the MOST appropriate manner for a counselor to assume during an interview with a patient is

    A. authoritarian
    B. paternal
    C. casual
    D. businesslike

25. _____

KEY (CORRECT ANSWERS)

1.	C	11.	A
2.	D	12.	C
3.	B	13.	B
4.	A	14.	B
5.	B	15.	D
6.	A	16.	B
7.	C	17.	A
8.	A	18.	D
9.	C	19.	A
10.	D	20.	C

21. A
22. C
23. B
24. C
25. D

TEST 2

DIRECTIONS: Each question or incomplete statement is followed by several suggested answers or completions. Select the one that *BEST* answers the question or completes the statement. *PRINT THE LETTER OF THE CORRECT ANSWER IN THE SPACE AT THE RIGHT.*

1. You are interviewing a legally responsible absent father who refuses to make child support payments because he claims the mother physically abuses the child.
   Of the following, the *BEST* way for you to handle this situation is to tell the father that you

   A. will report his complaint about the mother, but he is still responsible for making child support payments
   B. suspect that he is complaining about the mother in order to avoid his own responsibility for making child support payments
   C. are concerned with his responsibility to make child support payments, not with the mother's abuse of the child
   D. can not determine his responsibility for making child support payments until his complaint about the mother is investigated

   1.____

2. You are interviewing an elderly woman who lives alone to determine her eligibility for homemaker service at public expense. Though obviously frail and in need of this service, the woman is not completely cooperative, and during the interview, is often silent for a considerable period of time.
   Of the following, the *BEST* way for you to deal with these periods of silence is to

   A. realize that she may be embarrassed to have to apply for homemaker service at public expense, and emphasize her right to this service
   B. postpone the interview and make an appointment with her for a later date, when she may be better able to cooperate
   C. explain to the woman that you have many clients to interview and need her cooperation to complete the interview quickly
   D. recognize that she is probably hiding something and begin to ask questions to draw her out

   2.____

3. During a conference with an adolescent boy at a juvenile detention center, you find out for the first time that he would prefer to be placed in foster care rather than return to his natural parents.
   To uncover the reasons why the boy dislikes his own home, of the following, it would be *MOST* advisable for you to

   A. ask the boy a number of short, simple questions about his feelings
   B. encourage the boy to talk freely and express his feelings as best he can
   C. interview the parents and find out why the boy doesn't want to live at home
   D. administer a battery of psychological tests in order to make an assessment of the boy's problems

   3.____

4. You are interviewing a mother who is applying for Aid to Families with Dependent Children because the husband has deserted the family. The mother becomes annoyed at having to answer your questions and tells you to leave her apartment.
   Which one of the following actions would be *most appropriate* to take *FIRST* in this situation?

   4.____

A. Return to the office and close the case for lack of cooperation
B. Tell the mother that you will get the information from her neighbors if she does not cooperate
C. Tell the mother that you must stay until you get answers to your questions
D. Explain to the mother the reasons for the interview and the consequences of Her failure to cooperate

5. A counselor counseling juvenile clients finds that, although he can tolerate most of their behavior, he becomes infuriated when they lie to him.
   Of the following, the counselor can BEST deal with his anger at his clients' lying by

   A. recognizing his feelings of anger and learning to control expression of these feelings to his clients
   B. warning his clients that he cannot be responsible for his anger when a client lies to him
   C. using will power to suppress his feelings of anger when a client lies to him
   D. realizing that lying is a common trait of juveniles and not directed against him personally

6. During an interview, one of your clients, a former drug addict, has expressed an interest in attending a community counseling center and resuming his education.
   In this case, the MOST appropriate action that you should take FIRST is to

   A. determine whether this ambition is realistic for a former drug addict
   B. send the client's application to a community counseling center which provides services to former addicts
   C. ask the client whether he is really motivated or is just seeking your approval
   D. encourage and assist the client to take this step, since his interest is a positive sign

7. You are interviewing a client who, during previous appointments, has not responded to your requests for information required to determine his continued eligibility for services. On this occasion, the client again offers an excuse which you feel is not acceptable.
   For you to advise the client of the probable loss of services because of his lack of cooperation is

   A. *inappropriate,* because the threat to withhold services will harm the relationship between counselor and client
   B. *inappropriate,* because counselors should not reveal to clients that they do not believe their statements
   C. *appropriate,* because social services are a reward given to cooperative clients
   D. *appropriate,* beca,us.e the counselor should Inform clients of the consequences of their lack of cooperation

8. Assume that you are counselling an adolescent boy in a juvenile detention center who has been a ringleader in smuggling "pot" into the center.
   During your regular interview with this boy, of the following, it would be *advisable* to

   A. tell him you know that he has been involved in smuggling pot and that you are trying to understand the reasons for his misbehavior
   B. ignore his pot smuggling in order to reassure him that you understand and accept him, even though you do not agree with his standards of behavior
   C. warn him that you have reported his pot smuggling and that he will be punished for his misbehavior
   D. show him that you disapprove of his pot smuggling, but assure him that you will not report him for his misbehavior

9. Your unit has received several complaints about a homeless elderly woman living outdoors in various locations in the area. To help determine the need for protective services for this woman, you interview several persons in the neighborhood who are familiar with her, but all are uncooperative or reluctant to give information.
Of the following, your BEST approach to these persons is to explain to them that

   A. you will take legal steps against them if they do not cooperate with you
   B. their cooperation may enable you to help this homeless woman
   C. you need their cooperation to remove this homeless woman from their neighborhood
   D. they will be responsible for any harm that comes to this homeless woman

10. Assume that you are interviewing a client regarding an adjustment in budget. The client begins to scream at you that she holds you responsible for the decrease in her allowance.
Of the following, which is the BEST way for you to handle this situation?

   A. Attempt to discuss the matter calmly with the client and explain her right to a hearing.
   B. Urge the client to appeal and assure her of your support
   C. Tell the client that her disorderly behavior will be held against her
   D. Tell the client that the reduction is "due to red tape" and is not your fault

11. As a counselor assigned to a juvenile detention center, you are having a counselling interview with a recently admitted boy who is having serious problems in adjusting to confinement in the center. During the interview, the boy frequently interrupts to ask you personal questions. Of the following, the BEST way for you to deal with these questions is to

   A. tell him in a friendly way that your job is to discuss his problems, not yours
   B. try to understand how the questions relate to the boy's own problems and reply with discretion
   C. take no notice of the questions and continue with the interview
   D. try to win the boy's confidence by answering his questions in detail

12. A counselor is interviewing an elderly woman who hesitates to provide necessary information about her finances to determine whether she is eligible for supplementary assistance. She fears that this information will be reported to others and that her neighbors will find out that she is destitute and applying for "welfare." Of the following, the counselor's MOST appropriate response is to

   A. tell her that, if she hesitates to give this information, the agency will get it from other sources
   B. assure her that this information is kept strictly confidential and will not be given to unauthorized persons
   C. convince her that her application will be turned down unless she provides this information as soon as possible
   D. ask for the name and address of her nearest relative and obtain the information from that person

13. You are counseling a couple whose children have been placed in a foster home because of the couple's quarreling and child neglect. When you interview the wife by herself, she tells you that she knows the husband often "cheats" on her with other women, but she is too afraid of the husband's temper to tell him how much this hurts her.
For you to immediately reveal to the husband the wife's unhappiness concerning his "cheating" is, generally,

    A. *good practice,* because it will help the husband to understand why his wife quarrels with him
    B. *poor practice,* because information received from the wife should not be given to the husband without her permission
    C. *good practice,* because the husband will direct his anger at you rather than at his wife
    D. poor *practice,* because the wife may have told you a false story about her husband in order to win your sympathy

14. A counselor is beginning a job placement interview with a tall, strongly built young man. As the man sits down, the counselor comments: "I know a big fellow like you wouldn't be interested in any clerical job."
For the counselor to make such a comment is, generally,

    A. *appropriate,* because it creates an air of familiarity which may put the man at ease
    B. *inappropriate,* because the man may be sensitive about his physical size
    C. *appropriate,* because, the counselor is using his judgment to help speed up the interview
    D. *inappropriate,* because the man may feel he is being pressured into agreeing with the counselor

15. A counselor in a men's shelter is counseling a middle-aged client for alcoholism. During counseling, the" client confesses that, many years ago, he had often enjoyed sexually abusing his ten-year-old daughter. The counselor tells the client that he personally finds the client's behavior "morally disgusting."
For the counselor to tell the client this is, generally,

    A. *acceptable counseling practice,* because it may encourage the client to feel guilty about his behavior
    B. una*cceptable* cou*seling practice* , because the client may try to shock the counselor by confessing other similar behavior
    C. *acceptable counseling practice,* because "letting off steam" in this manner may relieve tension between the counselor and the client
    D. *unacceptable counseling practice,* because the client may hesitate to discuss his behavior frankly with the counselor in the future

16. During an interview, your client, who wants to move to a larger apartment, asks you to decide on a suitable neighborhood for her.
For you to make such a decision for the client would, generally, be considered

   A. *appropriate,* because you can save time and expense by sharing your knowledge of neighborhoods with the client
   B. *inappropriate,* because counselors should not help clients with this type of decision
   C. *appropriate,* because this will help the client to develop confidence in her ability to make decisions
   D. *inappropriate,* because the client should be encouraged to accept the responsibility of making this decision

17. A client tells you that he is extremely upset by the treatment that he received from Center personnel at the information desk.
Which of the following is the BEST way to handle this complaint during the interview?

   A. Explain to the client that he probably misinterpreted what occurred at the information desk
   B. Let the client express his feelings and then proceed with the interview
   C. Tell the client that you are not concerned with the personnel at the information desk
   D. Escort the client to the information desk to find out what really happened

18. You are finishing an interview with a client in which you have explained to her the procedure she must go through to apply for income maintenance.
Of the following, the BEST way for you to make sure that she has fully understood the procedure is to ask her

   A. whether she feels she has understood your explanation of the procedure
   B. whether she has any questions to ask you about the procedure
   C. to describe the procedure to you in her own words
   D. a few questions to test her understanding of the procedure

19. You are interviewing a client in his home as part of your investigation of an anonymous complaint that he has been receiving Medicaid fraudulently. During the interview, the client frequently interrupts your questions to discuss the hardships of his life and the bitterness he feels about his medical condition.
Of the following, the BEST way for you to deal with these discussions is to

   A. cut them off abruptly, since the client is probably just trying to avoid answering your questions
   B. listen patiently, since these discussions may be helpful to the client and may give you information for your investigation
   C. remind the client that you are investigating a complaint against him and he must answer directly
   D. seek to gain the client's confidence by discussing any personal or medical problems which you yourself may have

20. While interviewing an absent father to determine his ability to pay child supprt, you realize that his answers to some of your questions contradict his answers to other questions. Of the following, the *BEST* way for you to try to get accurate information from the father is to

    A. confront him with his contradictory answers and demand an explanation from him
    B. use your best judgment as to which of his answers are accurate and question him accordingly
    C. tell him that he has misunderstood your questions and that he must clarify his answers
    D. ask him the same questions in different words and follow up his answers with related questions

21. The one of the following types of interviewees who presents the *LEAST* difficult problem to handle is the person who

    A. answers with a great many qualifications
    B. talks at length about unrelated subjects so that the counselor cannot ask questions
    C. has difficulty understanding the counselor's vocabulary
    D. breaks into the middle of sentences and completes them with a meaning of his own

22. A man being interviewed is entitled to Medicaid, but he refuses to sign up for it because he says he cannot accept any form of welfare.
    Of the following, the *BEST* course of action to take *FIRST* is to

    A. try to discover the reason for his feeling this way
    B. tell him that he should be glad financial help is available
    C. explain that others cannot help him if he will not help himself
    D. suggest that he speak to someone who is already on Medicaid

23. Of the following, the outcome of an interview by a counselor depends *MOST* heavily on the

    A. personality of the interviewee
    B. personality of the counselor
    C. subject matter of the questions asked
    D. interaction between counselor and interviewee.

24. Some clients being interviewed are primarily interested in making a favorable impression. The counselor should be aware of the fact that such clients are *more likely* than other clients to

    A. try to anticipate the answers the interviewer is looking for
    B. answer all questions openly and frankly
    C. try to assume the role of interviewer
    D. be anxious to get the interview over as quickly as possible

25. The type of interview which a counselor usually conducts is substantially different from most interviewing situations in all of the following aspects *EXCEPT* the

    A. setting
    B. kinds of clients
    C. techniques employed
    D. kinds of problems

KEY (CORRECT ANSWERS)

1.	A	11.	B
2.	A	12.	B
3.	B	13.	B
4.	D	14.	D
5.	A	15.	D
6.	D	16.	D
7.	D	17.	B
8.	A	18.	C
9.	B	19.	B
10.	A	20.	D

21. C
22. A
23. D
24. A
25. C

EXAMINATION SECTION
TEST 1

DIRECTIONS: Each question or incomplete statement is followed by several suggested answers or completions. Select the one that BEST answers the question or completes the statement. *PRINT THE LETTER OF THE CORRECT ANSWER IN THE SPACE AT THE RIGHT.*

1. Which one of the following "suggestions to interviewers" should be AVOIDED? 1._____
   A. Encourage the client to verbalize his thoughts and feelings.
   B. Cover as much as possible in each interview.
   C. Don't hesitate to refer the client to someone else who might be more helpful in the situation.
   D. The problem which is presented initially, or the one which seems most obvious, often is not the real one.

2. If it seems clear that disturbance in parents' marital relationships is a major factor in causing a child to be emotionally disturbed, the counselor should 2._____
   A. point this out to the parents and tell them that for the welfare of their children, they should resolve their difficulties
   B. suggest that he will be willing to discuss their marital difficulties with them
   C. ignore this and concentrate on helping the child
   D. tactfully suggest that their marital difficulties may be playing a part in their child's disturbance and offer to refer the parents to a qualified marriage counseling service

3. The process of collecting, analyzing, synthesizing and interpreting information about the client should be 3._____
   A. completed prior to counseling
   B. completed early in the counseling process
   C. limited to counseling which is primarily diagnostic in purpose
   D. continuous throughout counseling

4. Catharsis, the "emotional unloading" of the client's feelings, has a value in the early stages of counseling because it accomplishes all BUT which one of the following goals? 4._____
   A. It relieves strong physiological tensions in the client.
   B. It increases the client's anxiety and therefore his motivation to continue counseling.
   C. It provides a verbal substitute for "acting out" the client's aggressive feelings.
   D. It releases emotional energy which the client has been using to maintain his defenses.

5. During the first interview, the counselor can expect the client to participate at his BEST when the counselor 5._____
   A. structures the nature of the counseling process
   B. attempts to summarize the client's problem for him
   C. allows the client to verbalize at his own pace
   D. tells the client that he understands the presenting problem

6. To obtain the most effective results in change of attitude and behavior through parent education, the leader should be

   A. thoroughly grounded in the whole field of psychology
   B. able to help members of the group look at their own attitudes and behavior in constructive ways
   C. completely confident as to the right solution to problems that may be brought up
   D. a warm, charming, friendly human being

6.____

7. A social worker's report about a client states that a mother has ambivalent feelings concerning her child. This means that the mother

   A. has contradictory emotional reactions concerning her child
   B. is overprotective of the child
   C. strongly rejects the child
   D. is unduly apprehensive about the child's welfare

7.____

8. A psychological report notes, "The client shows little effect." This means that the client

   A. did not take the test too seriously
   B. did not show emotional behavior in situations which normally call for such reactions
   C. did not show signs of fatigue as the testing progressed
   D. reacted to the test situation in a generally favorable manner

8.____

9. A psychologist's report states, in part, that a client exhibits some masochistic symptoms. This will be evident to the counselor through the client's persistent attempts at

   A. self-assertion
   B. self-effacement
   C. inflicting physical harm on others
   D. sexual molestation of others of the same sex

9.____

10. According to research studies, the type of counselor response that is MOST often followed by a client's expression of insight or illumination is

    A. clarification of feeling
    B. reflection of feeling
    C. simple acceptance
    D. exploratory question

10.____

11. Of the following, the BEST way to deal with a 12-year-old boy who feels inferior to his peers is to

    A. provide tasks which he can master with little difficulty
    B. show him how irrational his feelings are
    C. accept his declarations of lack of confidence sympathetically
    D. carefully arrange situations in which he will be obliged to show leadership

11.____

12. In counseling or psychotherapy, the factor which is the MOST important for success tends to be the

    A. counselor's theoretical orientation
    B. counselor's attitudes and feelings toward the client

12.____

C. techniques used by the counselor
D. amount of experience and training possessed by the counselor

13. Transference is an important aspect of   13.____

    A. test construction   B. grade placement
    C. anecdotal record keeping D. therapy

14. The MOST desirable way of establishing rapport with a client who comes to the counselor with a problem is to   14.____

    A. demonstrate sincere interest in him
    B. offer to do everything possible to solve his problem for him
    C. use the language of the client
    D. promise to keep his problem confidential

15. Role playing has been used as a technique in parent education work. Of the following, the major value is that it   15.____

    A. permits parents to express unconscious feelings and thereby solve conflicts
    B. tells a story in a forceful and therefore lasting way
    C. provides an opportunity for the individual to view his problems by standing off and looking at them through the eyes of someone else
    D. brings to light problems people never knew they had

16. If during a counseling situation a client expressed anger about a particular situation, which of the following responses would a non-directive counselor MOST likely make?   16.____

    A. "Why are you so angry?"
    B. "Is there any need to get so upset about this?"
    C. "This has really made you very mad, hasn't it?"
    D. "Do you feel better now that you have expressed your anger?"

17. In a counseling process, the counselor should usually give information   17.____

    A. whenever it is needed
    B. at the end of the process
    C. in the introductory interview
    D. just before the client would ordinarily request it

18. "After having recognized and clarified feelings and conflicts, it is usually necessary to go beyond the stage of understanding and to elaborate a constructive plan for future action." Which of the following people would NOT go along with the above statement?   18.____

    A. Thorne   B. Robinson
    C. Williamson   D. Rogers

19. The counselor should focus his attention in the beginning upon   19.____

    A. the transference phenomenon
    B. evidences of hostility
    C. the unique characteristics of the particular relationship at hand
    D. indications of client aggressiveness

20. A recent guidance text that stresses the broad developments of our national heritage, our contemporary social setting, our value patterns, and also the integration into guidance of many disciplines-sociology, anthropology, philosophy, psychology-is   20.____

   A. FOUNDATIONS OF GUIDANCE - Miller
   B. GUIDANCE POLICY AND PRACTICE - Mathewson
   C. GUIDANCE IN TODAY'S SCHOOLS - Mortenson & Schmuller
   D. GUIDANCE SERVICES - Humphreys, Traxler & North

21. Which one of the following characteristics of counseling is inconsistent with the others?   21.____

   A. Counseling is more than advice-giving.
   B. Counseling involves something more than the solution to an immediate problem.
   C. Counseling concerns itself with attitudes rather than actions.
   D. Counseling involves intellectual rather than emotional attitudes as its basic raw material.

22. One approach to counseling has been labeled "non-directive". The word "non-directive" derives from the fact that, in this approach to counseling, the counselor   22.____

   A. does not tell the client what he should do
   B. makes the client responsible for the direction of the course of the interviews
   C. does not make judgments about the behavior of the client
   D. avoids possible areas of threat to the client

23. Of the following personality traits, which would be LEAST essential for an effective counselor to possess?   23.____

   A. Extroversion   B. Objectivity
   C. Security   D. Sensitivity

24. Interpretation as a therapeutic tool is considered a hindrance to therapy progress by   24.____

   A. orthodox Freudians   B. neo-analysts
   C. Rogerians   D. Adlerians

25. The current interpersonal behavior of the client is probably MOST important as a therapy topic to which two analytic theorists?   25.____

   A. Freud and Adler   B. Adler and Rank
   C. Freud and Rank   D. Horney and Sullivan

KEY (CORRECT ANSWERS)

1.	B	11.	A
2.	D	12.	B
3.	D	13.	D
4.	B	14.	A
5.	C	15.	C
6.	B	16.	C
7.	A	17.	A
8.	B	18.	D
9.	B	19.	C
10.	C	20.	A

21. D
22. B
23. A
24. C
25. D

TEST 2

DIRECTIONS: Each question or incomplete statement is followed by several suggested answers or completions. Select the one that BEST answers the question or completes the statement. *PRINT THE LETTER OF THE CORRECT ANSWER IN THE SPACE AT THE RIGHT.*

1. When a counselor is listening to a client, it is MOST important that he be able to 1.____

    A. show interest and agreement with what the client is saying
    B. paraphrase what the client is saying
    C. understand the significance of what the client is saying
    D. differentiate between fact and fiction in what the client is saying

2. On which one of the following is successful counseling LEAST likely to depend? 2.____

    A. The counselor's theoretical orientation
    B. The counselor's ability to bring the client's feelings and attitudes into the open
    C. The counselor's diagnostic ability
    D. The client's readiness for counseling

3. A client is referred to you for counseling against his will and is suspicious and uncooperative. You should 3.____

    A. explain to him that you cannot help him unless he is prepared to cooperate
    B. explain that you are not taking sides and that you will be impartial
    C. show him that you know how he feels and encourage him to talk about it
    D. explain that you are on his side and will listen sympathetically to anything that he might care to bring up

4. Which one of the following would NOT be considered a basic objective of the first interview between a client and a counselor? 4.____

    A. Beginning a sound counseling relationship
    B. Identifying the client's real problem
    C. Opening up the area of client feelings and attitudes
    D. Clarifying the nature of the counseling process for the client

5. All of the following counselor statements or actions are appropriate techniques for ending an interview EXCEPT 5.____

    A. "Our time is nearly up. Is there something else you have in mind for today?"
    B. "Let's see now. Suppose we go over what we've accomplished today."
    C. Counselor may glance at his watch and say, "When would you like to come in again?"
    D. Counselor may shuffle papers on desk and say, "Now, let's see; when is my next appointment?"

6. It has been recognized in recent literature that the value structure of the individual counselor has what kind of effect on the counseling process? 6.____

    A. Direct
    B. Indirect
    C. Little
    D. None

7. The intensive study of the same individuals over a fairly long period of time represents the

   A. cross-sectional approach
   B. longitudinal approach
   C. clinical approach
   D. biographical approach

8. Of the following techniques, the one which is MOST characteristic of non-directive or client-centered therapy is

   A. encouraging transference
   B. free association
   C. reflection of feeling
   D. permissive questioning

9. In making predictions about how a client will behave in a given situation, a counselor

   A. should limit himself to those situations for which "actuarial" data are available
   B. must rely on "clinical" judgment in many situations but use "actuarial" data wherever possible
   C. should rely on "clinical" judgment in all situations, since they are more valid than "actuarial" predictions
   D. always uses "actuarial" data, but modifies them in light of his "clinical" impression of the client

10. A research study that establishes an hypothesis, sets up control groups, collects data, and generalizes from the data is

    A. formulative
    B. diagnostic
    C. experimental
    D. exploratory

11. The MOST usable single index of the social and economic status of all the members of any family is

    A. occupation of the father
    B. religious affiliation of the family
    C. location of the home in the community
    D. socio-economic rating by neighbors

12. When a counselor does NOT understand the meaning of a response that a counselee has made, the counselor usually should

    A. proceed to another topic
    B. admit his lack of understanding and ask for clarification
    C. act as if he understands so that the counselee's confidence in him is not shaken
    D. ask the counselee to choose his words more carefully

13. When the counselor makes a response which touches off a high degree of resistance in the counselee, he should

    A. apologize and rephrase his remark in a less threatening manner
    B. accept the resistance
    C. ignore the counselee's resistance
    D. recognize that little more will be accomplished in the interview and offer another appointment

14. Directive and non-directive counseling are two emphases in counseling theory and practice. From the pairs of names listed below, indicate the two that are representative of the Directive school.

 A. Thorne and Williamson
 B. Rogers and Thorne
 C. Williamson and Sullivan
 D. Sullivan and Rogers

15. Rogerian counseling theory is based on the assumption that the potential and tendency for growth toward a fully functioning personality is present in

 A. a few "self-actualized" persons
 B. most people of above average intelligence
 C. people whose behavior can be considered as "normal" and socially effective
 D. all people

16. Anecdotal records should contain which type(s) of information?

 A. Evaluations
 B. Interpretations
 C. Factual reports
 D. Prognoses

17. RESISTANCE in relation to psychological counseling typically refers to the

 A. client's defenses against his inner conflicts
 B. counselor's unwillingness to deal with the client's emotional problems
 C. client's having enough ego strength so that he can face his problems
 D. counselor's having enough ego strength so that he can help the client face his problems

18. On which one of the following does the democratic leader specifically rely? His ability to

 A. listen and tactfully guide the discussion in the direction he has planned and the members' willingness to cooperate
 B. diagnose situations, to interpret and explain them to the members and their willingness to accept
 C. discern the issues which the members could profitably discuss and his willingness to allow them with his help to do so
 D. understand the meaning of the response from the member's frame of reference and his willingness for them to make decisions

19. Advisement in counseling is MOST effective when the counselee is in a state of

 A. perceiving his problem as related to a conflict with inner forces
 B. minimal conflict and of optimal readiness for action
 C. perceiving his problem as related to an external conflict
 D. feeling extremely ambivalent about his self-concept

20. Of the following, the MOST valid use of projective techniques is the study of the

 A. problems which an individual faces
 B. cultural effects upon an individual
 C. inner world of an individual
 D. human relationships of an individual

21. Diagnosis is NOT regarded as a helpful antecedent to counseling by   21.____

    A. Cottle   B. Rogers
    C. Thorne   D. Williamson

22. The beginning counselor must be alert to interferences to rapport. Which one of the fol-   22.____
    lowing is NOT considered an intereference?

    A. Injecting the counselor's present mood
    B. Engaging in "small talk" at the start of the interview
    C. Registering surprise or dismay
    D. Emphasizing the counselor's ability

23. There is some evidence according to Rogers that counseling is more effective with   23.____

    A. younger adults or higher intelligence
    B. older adults of higher intelligence
    C. younger adults of lower intelligence
    D. older adults of lower intelligence

24. In assisting with the scheduling of interviews for educational planning, the counselor   24.____
    should suggest that group instruction

    A. follow the counseling interview
    B. is not necessary when individual interviews can be scheduled since each case is different
    C. precede the counseling
    D. may either precede or follow the counseling interview

25. A client has requested an interview with the counselor to discuss a personal problem. In   25.____
    general, the BEST way to begin the interview is to

    A. come directly to the point and encourage the client to talk about his problem
    B. assure him that everything discussed will be confidential
    C. offer to help him in every way possible
    D. inquire whether he has discussed the problem with anyone else

KEY (CORRECT ANSWERS)

1. C
2. A
3. C
4. B
5. D

6. A
7. B
8. C
9. B
10. C

11. A
12. B
13. B
14. A
15. D

16. C
17. A
18. C
19. B
20. C

21. B
22. B
23. A
24. C
25. A

PREPARING WRITTEN MATERIALS

EXAMINATION SECTION
TEST 1

DIRECTIONS: Each of the two sentences in the following questions may contain errors in punctuation, capitalization, or grammar.
If there is an error in only Sentence I, mark your answer A. If there is an error in only Sentence II, mark your answer B.
If there is an error in both Sentence I and Sentence II, mark your answer C. If both Sentence I and II are correct, mark your answer D.
PRINT THE LETTER OF THE CORRECT ANSWER IN THE SPACE AT THE RIGHT.

1. I. The task of typing these reports is to be divided equally between you and me. 1.____
   II. If it was he, I would use a different method for filing these records.

2. I. The new clerk is just as capable as some of the older employees, if not more capable. 2.____
   II. Using his knowledge of arithmetic to check the calculation, the supervisor found no errors in the report.

3. I. A typist who does consistently superior work probably merits promotion. 3.____
   II. In its report on the stenographic unit, the committee pointed out that neither the stenographers nor the typists were adequately trained.

4. I. Entering the office, the desk was noticed immediately by the visitor. 4.____
   II. Arrangements have been made to give this training to whoever applies for it.

5. I. The office manager estimates that this assignment, which is to be handled by you and I, will require about two weeks for completion. 5.____
   II. One of the recommendations of the report is that these kind of forms be discarded because they are of no value.

6. I. The supervisor knew that the typist was a quiet, cooperative, efficient, employee. 6.____
   II. The duties of stenographer are to take dictation notes at conferences and transcribing them.

7. I. The stenographer has learned that she, as well as two typists, is being assigned to the new unit. 7.____
   II. We do not know who you have designated to take charge of the new program.

8. I. He asked, "When do you expect to return?" 8.____
   II. I doubt whether this system will be successful here; it is not suitable for the work of our agency.

9. I. It is a policy of this agency to encourage punctuality as a good habit for we employees to adopt.
    II. The successful completion of the task was due largely to them cooperating effectively with the supervisor.

9.____

10. I. Mr. Smith, who is a very competent executive has offered his services to our department.
    II. Every one of the stenographers who work in this office is considered trustworthy.

10.____

11. I. It is very annoying to have a pencil sharpener, which is not in proper working order.
    II. The building watchman checked the door of Charlie's office and found that the lock has been jammed.

11.____

12. I. Since he went on the New York City council a year ago, one of his primary concerns has been safety in the streets.
    II. After waiting in the doorway for about 15 minutes, a black sedan appeared.

12.____

13. I. When you are studying a good textbook is important.
    II. He said he would divide the money equally between you and me.

13.____

14. I. The question is, "How can a large number of envelopes be sealed rapidly without the use of sealing machine?"
    II. The administrator assigned two stenographers, Mary and I, to the new bureau.

14.____

15. I. A dictionary, in addition to the office management textbooks, were placed on his desk.
    II. The concensus of opinion is that none of the employees should be required to work overtime.

15.____

16. I. Mr. Granger has demonstrated that he is as courageous, if not more courageous, than Mr. Brown.
    II. The successful completion of the project depends on the manager's accepting our advisory opinion.

16.____

17. I. Mr. Ames was in favor of issuing a set of rules and regulations for all of us employees to follow.
    II. It is inconceivable that the new clerk knows how to deal with that kind of correspondence.

17.____

18. I. The revised referrence manual is to be used by all of the employees.
    II. Mr. Johnson told Miss Kent and me to accumulate all the letters that we receive.

18.____

19. I. The supervisor said, that before any changes would be made in the attendance report, there must be ample justification for them.
    II. Each of them was asked to amend their preliminary report.

19.____

20. I. Mrs. Peters conferred with Mr. Roberts before she laid the papers on his desk.
    II. As far as this report is concerned, Mr. Williams always has and will be responsible for its preparation.

20.____

KEY (CORRECT ANSWERS)

1.	B	11.	C
2.	D	12.	C
3.	D	13.	A
4.	A	14.	B
5.	C	15.	C
6.	C	16.	A
7.	B	17.	B
8.	D	18.	A
9.	C	19.	C
10.	A	20.	B

TEST 2

DIRECTIONS: Each question or incomplete statement is followed by several suggested answers or completions. Select the one that BEST answers the question or completes the statement. *PRINT THE LETTER OF THE CORRECT ANSWER IN THE SPACE AT THE RIGHT.*

Questions 1-9.

DIRECTIONS: Questions 1 through 9 consist of pairs of sentences which may or may not contain errors in grammar, capitalization, or punctuation.
If both sentences are correct, mark your answer A.
If the first sentence only is correct, mark your answer B.
If the second sentence only is correct, mark your answer C.
If both sentences are incorrect, mark your answer D.
NOTE: Consider a sentence correct if it contains no errors, although there may be other correct ways of writing the sentence.

1. I. An unusual conference will be held today at George Washington high school. 1.____
    II. The principal of the school, Dr. Pace, described the meeting as "a unique opportunity for educators to exchange ideas.

2. I. Studio D, which they would ordinarily use, will be occupied at that time. 2.____
    II. Any other studio, which is properly equipped, may be used instead.

3. I. D.H. Lawrence's <u>Sons and Lovers</u> were discussed on today's program. 3.____
    II. Either Eliot's or Yeats's work is to be covered next week.

4. I. This program is on the air for three years now, and has a well-established audience. 4.____
    II. We have received many complimentary letters from listeners, and scarcely no critical ones.

5. I. Both Mr. Owen and Mr. Mitchell have addressed the group. 5.____
    II. As has Mr. Stone, whose talks have been especially well received.

6. I. The original program was different in several respects from the version that eventually went on the air. 6.____
    II. Each of the three announcers who Mr. Scott thought had had suitable experience was asked whether he would be willing to take on the special assignment.

7. I. A municipal broadcasting system provides extensive coverage of local events, but also reports national and international news. 7.____
    II. A detailed account of happenings in the South may be carried by a local station hundreds of miles away.

8. I. Jack Doe the announcer and I will be working on the program. 8.____
    II. The choice of musical selections has been left up to he and I.

9. I. Mr. Taylor assured us that "he did not anticipate any difficulty in making arrangements for the broadcast."
   II. Although there had seemed at first to be certain problems; these had been solved.

9.____

Questions 10-14.

DIRECTIONS: Questions 10 through 14 consist of pairs of sentences which may contain errors in grammar, sentence structure, punctuation, or spelling, or both sentences may be correct. Consider a sentence correct if it contains no errors, although there may be other correct ways of writing the sentence.
If only Sentence I contains an error, mark your answer A.
If only Sentence II contains an error, mark your answer B.
If both sentences contain errors, mark your answer C.
If both sentences are correct, mark your answer D.

10. I. No employee considered to be indispensable will be assigned to the new office.
    II. The arrangement of the desks and chairs give the office a neat appearance.

10.____

11. I. The recommendation, accompanied by a report, was delivered this morning.
    II. Mr. Green thought the procedure would facilitate his work; he knows better now.

11.____

12. I. Limiting the term "property" to tangible property, in the criminal mischief setting, accords with prior case law holding that only tangible property came within the purview of the offense of malicious mischief.
    II. Thus, a person who intentionally destroys the property of another, but under an honest belief that he has title to such property, cannot be convicted of criminal mischief under the Revised Penal Law.

12.____

13. I. Very early in its history, New York enacted statutes from time to time punishing, either as a felony or as a misdemeanor, malicious injuries to various kinds of property: piers, booms, dams, bridges, etc.
    II. The application of the statute is necessarily restricted to trespassory takings with larcenous intent: namely with intent permanently or virtually permanently to "appropriate" property or "deprive" the owner of its use.

13.____

14. I. Since the former Penal Law did not define the instruments of forgery in a general fashion, its crime of forgery was held to be narrower than the common law offense in this respect and to embrace only those instruments explicitly specified in the substantive provisions.
    II. After entering the barn through an open door for the purpose of stealing, it was closed by the defendants.

14.____

Questions 15-20.

DIRECTIONS: Questions 15 through 20 consist of pairs of sentences which may or may not contain errors in grammar, capitalization, or punctuation.
If both sentences are correct, mark your answer A.
If the first sentence only is correct, mark your answer B.
If the second sentence only is correct, mark your answer C.
If both sentences are incorrect, mark your answer D.
NOTE: Consider a sentence correct if it contains no errors, although there may be other ways of writing the sentence.

15. I. The program, which is currently most popular, is a news broadcast.
    II. The engineer assured his supervisor that there was no question of his being late again.

16. I. The announcer recommended that the program originally scheduled for that time be cancelled.
    II. Copies of the script may be given to whoever is interested.

17. I. A few months ago it looked like we would be able to broadcast the concert live.
    II. The program manager, as well as the announcers, were enthusiastic about the plan.

18. I. No speaker on the subject of education is more interesting than he.
    II. If he would have had the time, we would have scheduled him for a regular weekly broadcast.

19. I. This quartet, in its increasingly complex variations on a simple theme, admirably illustrates Professor Baker's point.
    II. Listeners interested in these kind of ideas will find his recently published study of Haydn rewarding.

20. I. The Commissioner's resignation at the end of next month marks the end of a long public service career.
    II. Outstanding among his numerous achievements were his successful implementation of several revolutionary schemes to reorganize the agency.

KEY (CORRECT ANSWERS)

1.	C	11.	D
2.	B	12.	C
3.	C	13.	B
4.	D	14.	A
5.	B	15.	C
6.	A	16.	A
7.	A	17.	D
8.	D	18.	B
9.	D	19.	B
10.	B	20.	B

PREPARING WRITTEN MATERIAL

PARAGRAPH REARRANGEMENT
COMMENTARY

The sentences that follow are in scrambled order. You are to rearrange them in proper order and indicate the letter choice containing the correct answer at the space at the right.

Each group of sentences in this section is actually a paragraph presented in scrambled order. Each sentence in the group has a place in that paragraph; no sentence is to be left out. You are to read each group of sentences and decide upon the best order in which to put the sentences so as to form a well-organized paragraph.

The questions in this section measure the ability to solve a problem when all the facts relevant to its solution are not given.

More specifically, certain positions of responsibility and authority require the employee to discover connection between events sometimes, apparently, unrelated. In order to do this, the employee will find it necessary to correctly infer that unspecified events have probably occurred or are likely to occur. This ability becomes especially important when action must be taken on incomplete information.

Accordingly, these questions require competitors to choose among several suggested alternatives, each of which presents a different sequential arrangement of the events. Competitors must choose the MOST logical of the suggested sequences.

In order to do so, they may be required to draw on general knowledge to infer missing concepts or events that are essential to sequencing the given events. Competitors should be careful to infer only what is essential to the sequence. The plausibility of the wrong alternatives will always require the inclusion of unlikely events or of additional chains of events which are NOT essential to sequencing the given events.

It's very important to remember that you are looking for the best of the four possible choices, and that the best choice of all may not even be one of the answers you're given to choose from.

There is no one right way to solve these problems. Many people have found it helpful to first write out the order of the sentences, as they would have arranged them, on their scrap paper before looking at the possible answers. If their optimum answer is there, this can save them some time. If it isn't, this method can still give insight into solving the problem. Others find it most helpful to just go through each of the possible choices, contrasting each as they go along. You should use whatever method feels comfortable and works for you.

While most of these types of questions are not that difficult, we've added a higher percentage of the difficult type, just to give you more practice. Usually there are only one or two questions on this section that contain such subtle distinctions that you're unable to answer confidently. And you then may find yourself stuck deciding between two possible choices, neither of which you're sure about.

EXAMINATION SECTION
TEST 1

DIRECTIONS: Each question consists of several sentences which can be arranged in a logical sequence. For each question, select the choice which places the numbered sentences in the MOST logical sequence. *PRINT THE LETTER OF THE CORRECT ANSWER IN THE SPACE AT THE RIGHT.*

1.
   I. A body was found in the woods.
   II. A man proclaimed innocence.
   III. The owner of a gun was located.
   IV. A gun was traced.
   V. The owner of a gun was questioned.
   The CORRECT answer is:
   A. IV, III, V, II, I
   B. II, I, IV, III, V
   C. I, IV, III, V, II
   D. I, III, V, II, IV
   E. I, II, IV, III, V

   1.____

2.
   I. A man is in a hunting accident.
   II. A man fell down a flight of steps.
   III. A man lost his vision in one eye.
   IV. A man broke his leg.
   V. A man had to walk with a cane.
   The CORRECT answer is:
   A. II, IV, V, I, III
   B. IV, V, I, III, II
   C. III, I, IV, V, II
   D. I, III, V, II, IV
   E. I, III, II, IV, V

   2.____

3.
   I. A man is offered a new job.
   II. A woman is offered a new job.
   III. A man works as a waiter.
   IV. A woman works as a waitress.
   V. A woman gives notice.
   The CORRECT answer is:
   A. IV, II, V, III, I
   B. IV, II, V, I, III
   C. II, IV, V, III, I
   D. III, I, IV, II, V
   E. IV, III, II, V, I

   3.____

4.
   I. A train let the station late.
   II. A man was late for work.
   III. A man lost his job.
   IV. Many people complained because the train was late.
   V. There was a traffic jam.
   The CORRECT answer is:
   A. V, II, I, IV, III
   B. V, I, IV, II, III
   C. V, I, II, IV, III
   D. I, V, IV, II, III
   E. II, I, IV, V, III

   4.____

5.
I. The burden of proof as to each issue is determined before trial and remains upon the same party throughout the trial.
II. The jury is at liberty to believe one witness' testimony as against a number of contradictory witnesses.
III. In a civil case, the party bearing the burden of proof is required to prove his contention by a fair preponderance of the evidence.
IV. However, it must be noted that a fair preponderance of evidence does not necessarily mean a greater number of witnesses.
V. The burden of proof is the burden which rests upon one of the parties to an action to persuade the trier of the facts, generally the jury, that a proposition he asserts is true.
VI. If the evidence is equally balanced, or if it leaves the jury in such doubt as to be unable to decide the controversy either way, judgment must be given against the party upon whom the burden of proof rests.
The CORRECT answer is:
  A. III, II, V, IV, I, VI   B. I, II, VI, V, III, IV   C. III, IV, V, I, II, VI
  D. V, I, III, VI, IV, II   E. I, V, III, VI, IV, II

5._____

6.
I. If a parent is without assets and is unemployed, he cannot be convicted of the crime of non-support of a child.
II. The term *sufficient ability* has been held to mean sufficient financial ability.
III. It does not matter if his unemployment is by choice or unavoidable circumstances.
IV. If he fails to take any steps at all, he may be liable to prosecution for endangering the welfare of a child.
V. Under the penal law, a parent is responsible for the support of his minor child only if the parent is of *sufficient ability*.
VI. An indigent parent may meet his obligation by borrowing money or by seeking aid under the provisions of the Social Welfare Law.
The CORRECT answer is:
  A. VI, I, V, III, II, IV   B. I, III, V, II, IV, VI   C. V, II, I, III, VI, IV
  D. I, VI, IV, V, II, III   E. II, V, I, III, VI, IV

6._____

7.
I. Consider, for example, the case of a rabble rouser who urges a group of twenty people to go out and break the windows of a nearby factory.
II. Therefore, the law fills the indicated gap with the crime of *inciting to riot*.
III. A person is considered guilty of inciting to riot when he urges ten or more persons to engage in tumultuous and violent conduct of a kind likely to create public alarm.
IV. However, if he has not obtained the cooperation of at least four people, he cannot be charged with unlawful assembly.
V. The charge of inciting to riot was added to the law to cover types of conduct which cannot be classified as either the crime of *riot* or the crime of *unlawful assembly*.
VI. If he acquires the acquiescence of at least four of them, he is guilty of unlawful assembly even if the project does not materialize.
The CORRECT answer is:
  A. III, V, I, VI, IV, II   B. V, I, IV, VI, II, III   C. III, IV, I, V, II, VI
  D. V, I, IV, VI, III, II   E. V, III, I, VI, IV, II

7._____

8. I. If, however, the rebuttal evidence presents an issue of credibility, it is for the jury to determine whether the presumption has, in fact, been destroyed.
    II. Once sufficient evidence to the contrary is introduced, the presumption disappears from the trial.
    III. The effect of a presumption is to place the burden upon the adversary to come forward with evidence to rebut the presumption.
    IV. When a presumption is overcome and ceases to exist in the case, the fact or facts which gave rise to the presumption still remain.
    V. Whether a presumption has been overcome is ordinarily a question for the court.
    VI. Such information may furnish a basis for a logical inference.
    The CORRECT answer is:
    A. IV, VI, II, V, I, III B. III, II, V, I, IV, VI C. V, III, VI, IV, II, I
    D. V, IV, I, II, VI, III E. II, III, V, I, IV, VI

9. I. An executive may answer a letter by writing his reply on the face of the letter itself instead of having a return letter typed.
    II. This procedure is efficient because it saves the executive's time, the typist's time, and saves office file space.
    III. Copying machines are used in small offices as well as large offices to save time and money in making brief replies to business letters.
    IV. A copy is made on a copying machine to go into the company files, while the original is mailed back to the sender.
    The CORRECT answer is:
    A. I, II, IV, III B. I, IV, II, III C. III, I, IV, II D. III, IV, II, I

10. I. Most organizations favor one of the types but always include the others to a lesser degree.
    II. However, we can detect a definite trend toward greater use of symbolic control.
    III. We suggest that our local police agencies are today primarily utilizing material control.
    IV. Control can be classified into three types: physical, material, and symbolic.
    The CORRECT answer is:
    A. IV, II, III, I B. II, I, IV, III C. III, IV, II, I D. IV, I, III, II

11. I. Project residents had first claim to this use, followed by surrounding neighborhood children.
    II. By contrast, recreation space within the project's interior was found to be used more often by both groups.
    III. Studies of the use of project grounds in many cities showed grounds left open for public use were neglected and unused, both by residents and by members of the surrounding community.
    IV. Project residents had clearly laid claim to the play spaces, setting up and enforcing unwritten rules for use.
    V. Each group, by experience, found their activities easily disrupted by other groups, and their claim to the use of space for recreation difficult to enforce.

The CORRECT answer is:
   A. IV, V, I, II, III   B. V, II, IV, III, I
   C. I, IV, III, II, V   D. III, V, II, IV, I

12.
    I. They do not consider the problems correctable within the existing subsidy formula and social policy of accepting all eligible applicants regardless of social behavior.
    II. A recent survey, however, indicated that tenants believe these problems correctable by local housing authorities and management within the existing financial formula.
    III. Many of the problems and complaints concerning public housing management and design have created resentment between the tenant and the landlord.
    IV. This same survey indicated that administrators and managers do not agree with the tenants.

    The CORRECT answer is:
       A. II, I, III, IV   B. I, III, IV, II   C. III, II, IV, I   D. IV, II, I, III

13.
    I. In single-family residences, there is usually enough distance between tenants to prevent occupants from annoying one another.
    II. For example, a certain small percentage of tenant families has one or more members addicted to alcohol.
    III. While managers believe in the right of individuals to live as they choose, the manager becomes concerned when the pattern of living jeopardizes others' rights.
    IV. Still others turn night into day, staging lusty entertainments which carry on into the hours when most tenants are trying to sleep.
    V. In apartment buildings, however, tenants live so closely together that any misbehavior can result in unpleasant living conditions.
    VI. Other families engage in violent argument.

    The CORRECT answer is:
       A. III, II, V, IV, VI, I   B. I, V, II, VI, IV, III
       C. II, V, IV, I, III, VI   D. IV, II, V, VI, III, I

14.
    I. Congress made the commitment explicit in the Housing Act of 194, establishing as a national goal the realization of a *decent home and suitable environment for every American family*.
    II. The result has been that the goal of decent home and suitable environment is still as far distant as ever for the disadvantaged urban family.
    III. In spite of this action by Congress, federal housing programs have continued to be fragmented and grossly underfunded.
    IV. The passage of the National Housing Act signaled a few federal commitment to provide housing for the nation's citizens.

    The CORRECT answer is:
       A. I, IV, III, II   B. IV, I, III, II   C. IV, I, II, III   D. II, IV, I, III

15. I. The greater expense does not necessarily involve *exploitation*, but it is often perceived as exploitative and unfair by those who are aware of the price differences involved, but unaware of operating costs.
  II. Ghetto residents believe they are *exploited* by local merchants, and evidence substantiates some of these beliefs.
  III. However, stores in low-income areas were more likely to be small independents, which could not achieve the economies available to supermarket chains and were, therefore, more likely to charge higher prices, and the customers were more likely to buy smaller-sized packages which are more expensive per unit of measure.
  IV. A study conducted in one city showed that distinctly higher prices were charged for goods sold in ghetto stores in other areas.
  The CORRECT answer is:
  A. IV, II, I, III   B. IV, I, III, II   C. II, IV, III, I   D. II, III, IV, I

15.____

KEY (CORRECT ANSWERS)

1.	C	6.	C	11.	D
2.	E	7.	A	12.	C
3.	B	8.	B	13.	B
4.	B	9.	C	14.	B
5.	D	10.	D	15.	C

BASIC QUESTIONS AND ANSWERS ON ALCOHOL

TABLE OF CONTENTS

		Page
Introduction		1
I.	What is alcohol?	1
II.	How does alcohol work in the body?	1
III.	How fast does alcohol take effect?	2
IV.	Why do people drink?	2
V.	What is drunkenness?	3
VI.	What is a hangover?	3
VII.	What physical harm can heavy drinking cause?	3
VIII.	How can you tell if someone is alcoholic?	4
IX.	How can a person with an alcohol problem be helped?	4
X.	Can alcohol problems be prevented?	5

BASIC QUESTIONS AND ANSWERS ON ALCOHOL

HOW WIDELY ARE ALCOHOLIC BEVERAGES USED?

As far back as historical records go, beverages containing alcohol have been made and used by people. Such beverages are part of the cultures of peoples throughout the world.

In fact, two-thirds of the adult population in the United States do drink at least occasionally, while one-third do not drink at all. Among the youth of this country, a recent survey found that most American adolescents have had at least some experience with alcoholic beverages. Almost 80 percent have had at least one drink; about 74 percent have had at least two or three drinks; and over one-half of all adolescents drink at least once a month.

I. WHAT IS ALCOHOL?

Alcohol, the major active ingredient in wine, beer, and distilled liquor, is a natural substance formed by the reaction of fermenting sugar with yeast spores. There are many alcohols, but the kind in alcoholic beverages is ethyl alcohol -- a colorless, inflammable liquid with an intoxicating effect.

Ethyl alcohol is a drug which can produce feelings of well-being, sedation, intoxication, or unconsciousness--depending on the amount and the manner in which it is drunk. Technically, it can also be classified as a food, since it contains calories; however, it has no nutritional value.

Various alcoholic beverages are produced by using different sources of sugar for fermentation. For instance, beer is made from grapes or berries, whiskey from malted trains, and rum from molasses. Hard liquors--such as whiskey, gin, and vodka--are produced by distillation, which further concentrates the alcohol resulting from fermentation.

ALCOHOL CONTENT OF TYPICAL ALCOHOLIC BEVERAGES

Beer - 4%
Dinner wine - 10-12%
Fortified wine - 17-20%
Distilled liquor - 40-50%

Each fluid ounce of 100 percent alcohol contains about 200 calories, although the alcoholic beverages and drinks derived from them vary widely. About the same alcoholic content, one-half ounce of pure alcohol, is found in:

a 12-ounce can of beer
a 5-ounce glass of dinner wine
a cocktail containing 1 1/2 ounces of 86-proof liquor

II. HOW DOES ALCOHOL WORK IN THE BODY?

Unlike other "food," alcohol does not have to be digested. When you drink an alcoholic beverage, 20 percent of the alcohol in it is absorbed immediately into the bloodstream through the stomach walls. The other 80 percent of the alcohol enters the bloodstream almost as fast after being quickly processed through the gastrointestinal tract. Moments after it is consumed, alcohol can be found in all tissues, organs, and secretions of the body. The alcohol eventually acts on the brain's central control areas to slow down or depress brain activity

A low level of alcohol in the blood, such as would result from sipping one drink--for example, a 12-ounce can of beer--has a mild tranquilzing effect on most people. Although basically a sedative, alcohol seems to act temporarily as a stimulant for many after they first start drinking. This is due to the fact that alcohol's initial effects are on those parts of the brain affecting learned behavior patterns such as self-control. After a drink or two, this learned behavior may temporarily disappear, making you lose your inhibitions, talk more freely, or feel like the "life of the party." On the other hand, you may feel aggressive or depressed.

Higher blood alcohol levels depress brain activity to the point that memory, as well as muscle coordination and balance, may be temporarily impaired. Still larger alcohol intake within a relatively short period of time depresses deeper parts of the brain, severely affecting judgment and dulling the senses.

If steady heavy drinking continues, the alcohol anesthetizes the deepest levels of the brain and can cause coma or death by depressing heart functions and breathing.

III. HOW FAST DOES ALCOHOL TAKE EFFECT?

The rapidity with which alcohol enters the bloodstream and exerts its effects on the brain and body depends on several factors:

How fast you drink. The half-ounce of pure alcohol in an average highball, can of beer, or glass of wine can be burned up or metabolized in the body in about 2 hours. If you sip your drink slowly and do not have more than one drink every 2 hours, the alcohol will not have a chance to jolt your brain or build up significantly in your blood, and you will feel little unpleasant effect. On the other hand, gulping drinks produces immediate, intoxicating effects and depression of deeper brain centers.

Whether your stomach is empty or full. Eating, especially before you drink but also while you drink, will slow down alcohol's rate of absorption into your bloodstream and produce a more even response to the alcohol.

What you drink. The alcohol in wine and beer is more diluted and is, therefore, absorbed somewhat more slowly into the bloodstream than alcohol from hard liquor. Diluting distilled spirits with water also helps to slow down absorption, but mixing with carbonated beverages can increase the rate of absorption.

How much you weigh. The effect of alcohol on the body varies according to a person's weight. Alcohol is quickly distributed uniformly within the circulatory system. Therefore, if the same amount is drunk by a 120-pound person and a 180-pound person, the alcohol is more concentrated in the bloodstream of the lighter individual and therefore more intoxicating to that person.

The setting, your mood or expectations. If you are sitting down relaxed while having a drink with a friend, alcohol will not affect you as much as when you are standing and drinking at a cocktail party. If you are emotionally upset, under stress, or tired, alcohol may have a stronger impact on you than normal. Your expectations will also have an influence. If you think you are going to become drunk, you are likely to get that way more quickly.

IV. WHY DO PEOPLE DRINK?

People drink for a variety of social, cultural, religious, or medical reasons. They drink at parties and celebrations with friends and relatives. They drink in religious ceremonies. Some drink wine to complement the taste of their dinners. Some drink to relax. Some drink to increase their appetites.

The drinking of most people is "integrative" drinking; that is, the use of alcohol is an adjunct to other activities, such as meals, family and religious feasts, or an evening with friends.

Among Orthodox Jews, native Italians, and other groups where alcohol is part of religious or social traditions, there is a low incidence of problem drinking, though there is almost universal use of alcoholic beverages.

There are, however, large numbers of people who drink for reasons that are not social, cultural, religious, or medical. They use alcohol to forget their worries, to escape from reality, or to gather courage to face the stresses of life. They are using alcohol as a drug and are in danger of becoming dependent upon it.

V. WHAT IS DRUNKENNESS?

Drunkenness is characterized by a temporary loss of control over physical and mental powers caused by excessive alcohol intake. Symp-toms of drunkenness vary, but they can include impaired vision, distorted depth perception, thick speech, and bad coordination. The ability to solve problems is reduced, emotion and mood become unpredictable, memory is impaired, and judgment becomes poor.

In most States a person is considered legally drunk when he or she has a 0.10 percent blood alcohol level. This means that one part in every thousand parts of the person's blood is presently composed of pure alcohol. Such a situation generally results when a person weighing about 160 pounds has had about seven drinks within 2 hours after eating. A person will reach this stage with fewer drinks if body weight is less than 160 pounds, with more drinks if weight exceeds this fugure. In a few States, the legally drunk level is 0.15 percent. In either case, it is illegal to drive a car after the specified blood alcohol concentration is reached.

Contrary to a widespread impression, one cannot sober up by such devices as drinking black coffee, taking a cold shower, or breathing pure oxygen. It takes a specific amount of time for the body to burn up a quantity of alcohol, generally at the rate of 7 grams (about 1/4 ounce) of pure alcohol per hour. The effect of drinking alcohol can be varied only by controlling the rate and concentration with which it is drunk. Once alcohol is in the bloodstream, nothing can be done about its effects except to wait until it is metabolized by the body.

VI. WHAT IS A HANGOVER?

A hangover is the body's reaction to excessive drinking. The associated miseries of nausea, gastritis, anxiety, and headache vary from case to case, but there is always extreme fatigue. No scientific evidence supports the curative claims for coffee, raw eggs, oxysters, chili peppers, steak sauce, vitamins or other drugs, or the "hair of the dog." Doctors ususally prescribe aspirin, rest, and solid food.

If you choose to drink, the best way to avoid a hangover is to avoid drunkenness. Sip slowly, with food in the stomach, under relaxed circumstances, and pay attention to your responses to the alcohol so you don't drink too much.

VII. WHAT PHYSICAL HARM CAN HEAVY DRINKING CAUSE?

Heavy drinking over time can cause severe physiological damage. Cirrhosis of the liver is closely linked to heavy, continuous consumption of alcohol, and there is also a link between this type of drinking and ulcers, heart disease, and diabetes. Heavy drinking over many years may also contribute to serious nervous or mental disorders, or may cause permanent brain damage. Alcohol, like many other drugs that affect the central nervous system, can be physiologically addictive, producing withdrawal symptoms when alcohol intake ceases.

Of course, drinking need not be long-term or addictive to cause accidental injury or death. Only two cans of beer or two drinks of 86-proof whiskey consumed by the average 160-pound person within an hour on an empty stomach generally result in a blood alcohol level of 0.05 percent—one part of alcohol in every 2,000 parts of blood. Scientific studies have revealed that even these small amounts limit coordination and increase a person's risk of becoming involved in a traffic or household accident. This often comes as a surprise to people being tested, since many feel more capable and mentally alert than they did before drinking.

VIII. HOW CAN YOU TELL IF SOMEONE IS ALCOHOLIC?

Alcoholism is marked by dependence on alcohol and loss of control over one's drinking. This loss of control may develop almost imperceptibly over a long period, or it may manifest itself almost from the start of a person's drinking. When a person continues to drink despite the fact that it causes serious psychological, physical, or social problems, alcoholism is developing or is already present.

We tend to think of "typical" alcohol people as skid row inhabitants, but only about 3-5 percent of alcoholic Americans are in that category. Actually, alcoholic people represent a cross-section of America, embracing rich and poor, young and old, white-collar workers and blue-collar workers--in fact, every level of society. Most alcoholics are employed and most have families--much like their neighbors and fellow citizens.

Seldom can you spot alcoholic people by their appearance. However, for those close to a person who seems to be more and more dependent on alcohol in order to function, there are indicators that his or her drinking may be reaching the danger point. For example is there the immediate reaction to pour a drink when faced with any problem; has getting drunk become a regular occurrence; is there a record of missing work because of drinking or regular attendance at work with an ill-disguised odor of liquor on the breath; has the person's license been suspended for driving while drunk; has the person gotten into trouble with authorities for no "logical" reason; has the person been involved in several unexplainable accidents without evidence of physical impairment; has his or her home life become intolerable because of excessive drinking or arguments resulting from drinking?

When such signs are present, it means that a person's drinking pattern, if not already out of control, is heading that way.

IX. HOW CAN A PERSON WITH AN ALCOHOL PROBLEM BE HELPED?

In the past, most people believed that nothing could be done for a person with a drinking problem. It is now recognized that the overwhelming number can be helped at any stage so long as adequate treatment and rehabilitation resources are available, care is marked by acceptance and understanding, and the stigma of having an alcohol problem is not allowed to stand in the way of treatment.

Help can be provided by a doctor, a clergyman, a local welfare agency, a clinic, a social worker, a psychologist or psychiatrist, a general hospital or psychiatric hospital, an alcoholism treatment cen-ter, or the local chapter of Alcoholics Anonymous. Many large business or industrial firms and labor unions also have programs to help their alcoholic employees and members find treatment and rehabilitation.

Alcoholics Anonymous is probably the best known source of help for alcoholic persons. This organization is a self-help group in which members help each other in a type of group therapy setting that utilizes mutual experience for mutual support. Alcoholics Anonymous is listed in all local directories.

Other community and social agencies also offer referral services or direct help. Local affiliates of the National Council on Alcoholism exist in many communities, and every State and many communities have official alcoholism programs where help can be found or sources of treatment recommended. Again, the local telephone directory is the key to obtaining their services.

The treatment used for alcoholism is as varied as the reasons for alcoholic drinking, and programs which individualize the treatment approaches to the patient's needs offer the best results. Doctors may prescribe a drug, Antabuse, which makes an alcoholic person violently ill if he or she drinks alcohol. Psychotherapy and counseling may be used to provide long-range help. Although considerable success has been reported in nonmedical, social setting withdrawal from alcohol, in the case of acute alcoholism or acute intoxication, hospitalization may be required for a short period of time.

The primary goal of treatment is to help the person overcome his dependence on alcohol and develop a lifestyle not revolving around its use. Experience to date has been that the chances of improvement seem greatest if total abstinence is the goal. As many as two-thirds of the people who seek help recover from alcoholism, a figure that compares favorably with the results of treatment for other psychological or behavioral problems.

It is almost universally recognized today that alcoholism affects others besides the alcoholic individual--especially those close to the drinker. To meet this need, Al-Anon Family Groups were set up to assist the families--principally spouses--and more recently Alateen came into existence to help the adolescent children of alcoholic persons.

X. CAN ALCOHOL PROBLEMS BE PREVENTED?

Problem drinking and alcoholism can never be controlled solely by treating people. The long-range goal must be prevention; and this requires education, both in the schools and in the adult community, to develop the Nation's habits of moderation in the use of alcoholic beverages and to encourage respect for those who choose to abstain. It also requires investigation and testing of such social policies as control of distribution and availability, excise taxes, etc., as well as study of the effective prevention policies of other cultures.

One immediate step that we as individuals can take toward preventing alcohol problems in our own social circles is assuming the responsibilities that we as hosts and hostesses have to our friends. At dinner parties and social gatherings, food should be served both before and with drinks. As an alternative to alcoholic beverages, soft drinks--including low-calorie beverages--should be made available. These can be supplemented by nonalcoholic punches, fruit juices, tea, and coffee. The guest who does not choose to drink alcoholic beverages should never be cajoled or shamed into doing so, whether he is an abstainer, a recovered alcoholic, or a social drinker who recognizes he has had enough. One effective method of giving your guests some extra time for alcohol effects to wear off is to close the bar at least 1 or 2 hours before you plan to break up your party. This is the time to drink coffee and other nonalcoholic beverages and to serve your own special highlight dish of meat or seafood.

BASIC FUNDAMENTALS OF ALCOHOL AND ALCOHOLISM

TABLE OF CONTENTS

	Page
Introduction	1
I. Alcohol, the Beverage	1
II. Physiological Effects	2
III. Alcoholism Defined	4
IV. Alcoholism: Types	5
V. Causes of Alcoholism	6
VI. Tolerance	8
VII. Progressive Symptoms	9
VIII. Treatment	12
A. Emergency Treatment	12
B. Inpatient Treatment	14
C. Follow-up Treatment	15
D. Deterrent Therapy	16
E. Miscellaneous Therapies	17
F. Alcoholics Anonymous	18

BASIC FUNDAMENTALS OF ALCOHOL AND ALCOHOLISM

INTRODUCTION

"We deal with alcohol -- cunning, baffling, powerful," says the "Big Book" of Alcoholics Anonymous.

So be it. But the cunning, bafflement and power have often been embellished, by those who exploit it for their own ends. "Grab for all the gusto you can get!" urges the beer advertisement. "There's death in the cup -- so beware!" warns the tectotalist.

As a result, so many prejudices and old wives tales have been fostered by alcohol and alcoholism that John Doe has found himself groping in a fog of misunderstanding.

The alcoholism counselor, if he is to function effectively, must cut through the smoke screens and camouflage. Only in that way can he distinguish the true from the false and win the confidence of his patients, their families and their associates. And once he feels reasonably informed, there will be new facts and findings to assimilate and adapt to as research keeps marching on.

I. ALCOHOL, THE BEVERAGE

The history of man's use of alcohol may be boiled down to two sentences. Historically, there is every evidence that man learned how to brew beer before he learned how to bake bread. Go we have had alcohol, the beverage, with us through the ages and will probably continue to have it to the end of time -- legislation and condemnation notwithstanding.

The alcohol contained in the beverage alcohol is called ethyl alcohol (C_2H_5OH), also known as ethanol. There are many other types of alcohol -- such as methyl or wood alcohol, isopropyl or rubbing alcohol, both unfit for human consumption.

First, to examine some popular misconceptions:

Alcohol is <u>not</u> a stimulant. On the contrary, it is an anesthetic. As explained in the next section, it puts judgment and inhibitions to sleep so that emotions and desires are allowed to function unrestrained, giving a false sense of stimulation.

Alcohol is <u>not</u> an aphrodisiac, it does not stimulate one's appetite for sex. Although one or two drinks may lower the individual's inhibitions and facilitate the expression of repressed sexual desires, in larger amounts alcohol -- being an anesthetic -- tends to curb sexual desire and, in the male, may even impair his ability to perform.

Alcohol <u>is</u> an addictive drug. As with all other addictive drugs, the excessive use of alcohol leads to an increased tolerance for it. In the early stages of the disease, the alcoholic can consume much more than the non-alcoholic. Also, withdrawal symptoms often occur with abstinence. One of the more widely known examples is delirium tremens. However, it must be stressed that, as with all other addictive drugs, not all users become addicted. In the case of alcohol, only about 6 to 7 per cent of all drinkers become alcoholics.

Alcohol does <u>not</u> necessarily stimulate one's appetite for food. As a sedative, alcohol taken in small quantity before a meal may help one "unwind" and thus add to his enjoyment of the food by temporarily alleviating his emotional frustrations and worries. Some drinks (aperitifs) contain substances (strychnine, quinine, etc.) specifically for the appetite stimulating effects. In larger amounts, it suppresses the appetite, because one ounce of alcohol supplies 200 calories to the body. As a result, a heavy drinker may forego meals and rely on alcohol for his needed energy. But alcohol is a very poor substitute for food since it does not supply the proteins, vitamins and minerals necessary to good health.

Drinking in moderation does <u>not</u> in itself cause disease. But prolonged, excessive use of alcohol may lead to illnesses in several ways. They can be the direct result of the toxic effects of the drug on living tissue -- e.g., fatty deposits in the liver, heart muscle, etc. They can be the result of poor nutrition -- the lack of proteins, vitamins and minerals mentioned above. Or they can be the result of lowered resistance to infectious diseases -- i.e., the inhibition of the antibody building, defense mechanisms of the body.

By itself, alcohol is <u>not</u> a killer. It is virtually impossible for a man to deliberately "drink himself to death." When the concentration of alcohol in the blood reaches .50 per cent, it affects the portion of the brain that controls breathing and heartbeat, and death follows. But the drinker loses consciousness when the concentration reaches .40 per cent, at which point he can drink no more.

There is no alcoholic "drink of moderation." Beer, wine, and spirits all contain alcohol. It may take more beer (4%) than 100 proof whiskey (50%) to reach the same state of intoxication. But the effect of the alcohol is the same. The "moderation" rests in the drinker.

II. <u>PHYSIOLOGICAL EFFECTS</u>

When one takes a drink -- be it man or woman, alcoholic or non-alcoholic -- the brain and body respond in a systematic manner.

About 10 percent of the alcohol is eliminated through the lungs, kidneys and pores of the skin. The remaining 90 percent is directly absorbed into the blood stream through the walls of the stomach and small intestine. No other digestive processes are involved.

Once in the blood stream, it is distributed to the body tissues.

En route, the alcohol passes through the liver, where it is oxidized and transformed into energy. But even a healthy liver can only oxidize about three-quarters of an ounce per hour. So the excess accumulates in the blood and continues to circulate.

In the blood, alcohol reaches the brain. Here it has a sedative and an anesthetic effect.

The first part of the brain to be affected is the frontal lobe of the cerebrum. This is the seat of reasoning, conscious thinking, memory, self-control. As the frontal lobe is gradually anesthetized by the alcohol, inhibitions disappear. The man forgets his limitations and becomes Mr. Big. No transient ambition is beyond his capacities. The anxieties of day-to-day living evaporate and the world is his friend. This is the false "stimulation" referred to before.

As the concentration of alcohol in the blood increases, other areas of the brain are affected. The motor area of the cerebrum and the cerebellum control motor activity, muscular coordination and equilibrium. The drinker becomes clumsy and he begins to have trouble walking and keeping his balance. The speech, hearing and vision centers of the brain become affected, which result in slurred speech, dulled hearing and blurred vision. When the sensory area is affected the drinker "feels no pain," thus being deprived of a frequently lifesaving alarm system.

Finally, the medulla -- the portion of the brain connected to the spinal cord -- is affected. This is responsible for the vital functions of the body, including heartbeat, blood flow and breathing. Depending upon the concentration of the alcohol, the drinker will lose consciousness, go into shock, or die.

Thus a drinker's behavior and capabilities are directly related to the alcoholic concentration in his bloodstream. Such being the case, the drinking "capacity" of one man can vary from that of the next. The body fluids inside a 250-pound mailroom clerk. Other things being equal, more alcohol is required to raise the football player's concentration to .40%, or to any other given degree. So the amount of liquor considered "excessive" for one man may not be "excessive" for the next.

But football player or mailroom clerk, a drinker's behavior pattern generally conforms to the following levels of concentration:

.06% Feeling of warmth, relaxation, less concern with minor irritations.

.08% Legal point of intoxication

.09% Buoyancy, exaggerated emotion and behavior, talkative or morose.

.12% Impairment of fine coordination, slight to moderate unsteadiness in standing or walking.

.15% Abnormality of gross bodily function and mental facilities

.30% Stupor

.40% Unconsciousness, possible state of shock

.50% Death

There are, of course, other physiological effects resulting from drinking, many of which are noted below, under "Progressive Symptoms."

Both alcoholics and non-alcoholics, however, are liable to suffer irritation of the throat, esophagus and stomach lining through excessive drinking of undiluted liquors. Painful alcoholic gastritis can result from the latter

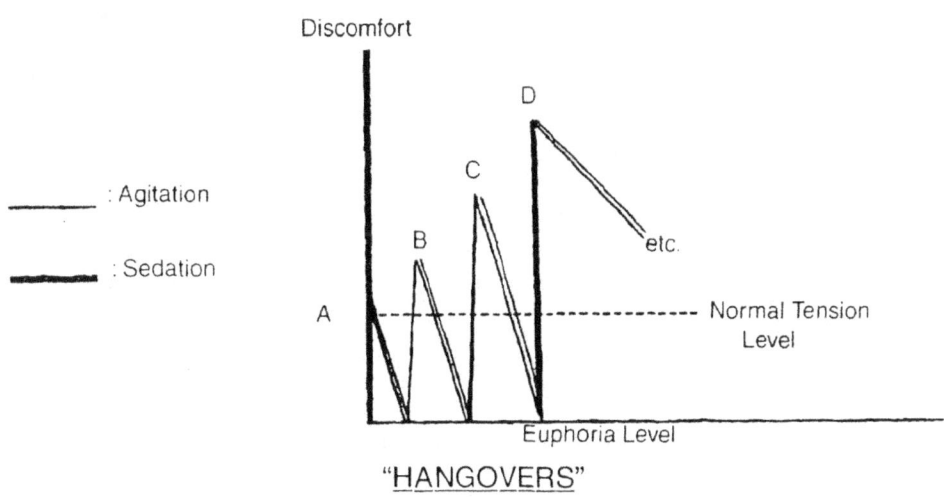

"HANGOVERS"

Then there is that transient hell through which any drinker can pass after he has imbibed too much "the hangover."

All sedatives, including alcohol, have a double-barreled effect. One is the tranquilizing effect which causes men and women to drink. The other is an irritating effect resulting in "psychomotor hyperactivity" which lasts many hours longer and which accounts for the "morning after" distress.

In the accompanying schematic diagram, assume that a man on his way to a party is somewhat nervous and normally anxious (point "A"). He takes a stiff drink to alleviate his anxiety and induce a sense of euphoria. At this stage the sedative effect of the alcohol is intense enough to mask the agitating effect. But within a relatively short period of time, the sedative effect of the alcohol is gone and he is left with only the psychomotor agitation, which gradually accelerates to point "B." He decides upon another drink to rectify matters. Now he needs even more sedation -- first, to get back to his normal state, and then more to become euphoric again. So the process of alternating sedation and agitation continues to points "C," "D" and so on -- until he either goes to bed himself or is carried there by his friends.

In actuality, the party-goer would surely refuel at the first suspicion that his euphoria was wearing off. But he would still awaken the following morning with an accumulation of the agitating effects of his drinks, which last about twelve hours from the time of imbibing. He has three choices: to sweat them out; to take a milder sedative to allay some of the pain; or to have some "hair bf the dog that bit him." The last is rather dangerous. He might find himself back on the same merry-go-round again.

III. ALCOHOLISM DEFINED

Thus far everything has applied to all the men and women who drink any alcoholic beverages at all.

What about the alcoholic? What about the 6 to 7 per cent of those drinkers -- the 1 out of 14 or 15 -- who have lost control of their drinking? What distinguishes them from the others?

There are hundreds of definitions of alcoholism. The technical one published by the World Health Organization reads as follows:

"Any form of drinking which in its extent goes beyond the traditional and customary 'dietary' use or the ordinary compliance with the social drinking customs of the whole community concerned, irrespective of the etiological factors leading to such behavior, and irrespective also of the extent to which such etiological factors are dependent upon heredity, constitution, or acquired physio-pathological and metabolic influences."

Shorter descriptions of the alcoholic include:

"One who repeatedly seeks to change reality through the use of alcohol."

Or

"One who suffers because of uncontrolled compulsive drinking."

For the alcoholism counselor, the following definition may serve as a useful yardstick in evaluating a client's status:

"An alcoholic is one whose drinking interferes with his health, his job, his relations with his family, or his community relationships and yet he continues to drink."

The interference need only be felt in one of the above areas of living for a person's classification as an alcoholic.

The fact that the alcoholic "continues to drink" implies loss of control, which is a characteristic of the illness.

The definition applies to men and women alike. Although it was once thought that male alcoholics outnumbered female alcoholics about five to one, it is now agreed that the number of women is much closer to that of men. Many private physicians who treat both men and women alcoholics say the ratio is about fifty-fifty.

And the definition applies to all social and economic "classes." Only 3 per cent of the alcoholics in the United States are found on Skid Row. The other 97 per cent stretch from waterfront saloons to Main Street and the Hall of Congress.

IV. ALCOHOLISM: TYPES

Since the alcoholic is usually the last to recognize his illness, he often challenges the doctor or counselor with:

"I only drink weekends (or paydays)!" or

"I can go months without touching a drop!" etc.

Such protests may be true. Nevertheless, he can still fall into one of the classifications of alcoholics that have been arrived at by many specialists in the field.

Probably the best known classification is that of the late Dr. E. M. Jellinek, former consultant to the World Health Organization. He identified various types of alcoholics with Greek letters:

<u>Alpha:</u> This man or woman relies upon the effect of alcohol to boost morale, bolster self-confidence or relieve emotional pain. He might be regarded as a "social drinker" except for the fact that he often drinks too much at the wrong times, among the wrong people, and is thereby apt to affront others.

The Alpha type does not lose control and can abstain when necessary. However, his drinking can give rise to family squabbles, occasional absenteeism from work, and be a drain on the family budget.

Alpha drinkers may develop into full-fledged Gamma alcoholics (see below). Hence, they are considered by many to be "pre-alcoholics," and should be treated accordingly to forestall that possibility.

Beta: This alcoholic gets sick. He does not become addicted and he suffers no withdrawal symptoms if he stops in tine.

But his poor nutritional habits -- i.e., substituting alcohol for necessary proteins, minerals and vitamins -- lead to such medical complications as peripheral neuritis, cirrhosis of the liver and gastritis. When hospitalized his ailments are all too often treated without regard to the drinking habits that have caused them.

Gamma: These are the alcoholics who most frequently need help from alcoholism clinics and such organizations as Alcoholics Anonymous. Their psychological dependence upon alcohol has grown into a physical dependence. They have lost control over their drinking, and they suffer withdrawal symptoms when they abstain. In early and middle stages of the illness, their tolerance for alcohol is much greater than that of the non-alcoholic. But in late stages their tolerance abruptly decreases to the point where even a single drink can make them ill. (See "Tolerance" and "Progressive Symptoms," below.)

Delta: The Delta alcoholic maintains a steady concentration of alcohol in his bloodstream during his waking hours. Usually he has grown up where alcohol is an all-purpose beverage, served at all meals. But he can be a business executive whose eye openers and three-martinis-for-lunch have become a ritual, or "the little old lady" whose daily quota of dry sherry is a must. Seldom visibly intoxicated, the Delta alcoholic will suffer withdrawal symptoms when forced to abstain. For example, when hospitalized for several days prior to surgery, they may develop delerium tremens.

Epsilon: This is the so called binge drinker, who will go for a long period weeks, months, or even a year without a drink. But once he starts, it is explosive. He continues drinking until he goes into a stupor. If the binges continue with increasing frequency, he may become a Gamma alcoholic.

Dr. Jellinek wrote that there are many other types of alcoholism, more than there are letters in the Greek alphabet. But the above five are the ones the alcoholism counselor is most likely to encounter.

Despite the protests of many alcoholics -- particularly the Gammas, Deltas, and Epsilons -- that they "can take it or leave it" or "only drink on payday," there is one common denominator. Consciously or subconsciously, they are forever looking forward and planning for the next drink, be it tomorrow, next week, or six months from now. This is not conducive to the "comfortable sobriety" that leads to recovery.

V. CAUSES OF ALCOHOLISM

Those engaged in scientific research have yet to establish that there is any hereditary influence in a person's susceptibility to alcohol addiction.

Nor is there any physical basis for alcoholism. However, as already noted, there can be a growing physiological dependence upon alcohol as the disease progresses.

Psychological and personality factors play an important role.

While heredity apparently has no part in determining the possibilities of a youngster's becoming an alcoholic in later years, his environment can. Many surveys indicate that about half the adult alcoholics interviewed have at least one alcoholic parent. Other children may be so repelled by the ugly topsyturvydom of parental drinking that they go through life without touching a drop although they may suffer other emotionally crippling effects.

CHILDHOOD EXPERIENCES

More important is the manner in which the child is taught to face reality. As the accompanying "Childhood Experiences" chart indicates, the "normal" child with "normal" parents sees them tackle the problems and decisions in everyday living as they arise. Other things being equal, he will do the same with his lesser difficulties and continue to do so with the big ones in adulthood.

But if the parents overdiscipline, overprotect or overindulge him, he will be more apt to shy away when confronted by any situation that demands his decision or constructive action. Later in life, he discovers that alcohol offers him temporary escape. This discovery eventually leads into habit. As he takes flight in the bottle more and more often, he can develop such a physiological dependency upon it that he is well on the way to full-fledged alcoholism.

The same liability faces the rejected child. Knowing he is not wanted, he is bound to feel a sense of inadequacy. Unless that is overcome, his so called solution to his problems may eventually be the same.

Of course, all alcoholics did not start out in life as overdisciplined, overprotected, overindulged or rejected children. The death of a loved one,

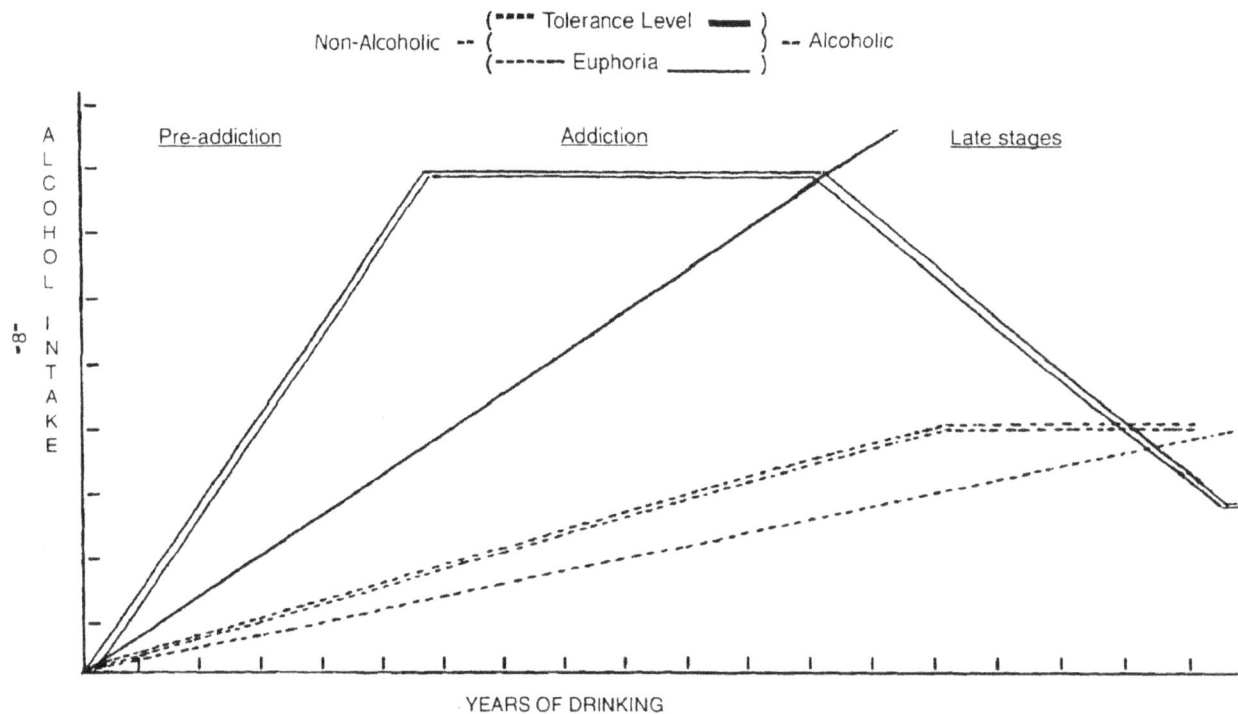

ALCOHOLIC AND NON-ALCOHOLIC TOLERANCE CURVES

unavoidable hard times, another's disloyalty, incessant physical pain, etc., can provoke feelings of inadequacy or frustration at any time from the nursery to the grave. When a person repeatedly turns to alcohol as an escape from his anxieties, great or small, he becomes a potential alcoholic.

In short, the onset of alcoholism is not determined by how much a man drinks, but why he drinks.

VI. TOLERANCE

Once embarked, the alcoholic's course is irreversibly charted -- unless he turns to total abstinence at some point along the way. In that case, he can arrest the progress of his illness. He cannot turn back. He cannot retrim his sails for social drinking.

The accompanying diagram of "Alcoholic and Non-Alcoholic Tolerance" indicates the general course the illness takes.

The "alcohol intake" level refers to the amount consumed at any one occasion. As noted above, what is excessive intake for one person is not necessarily excessive for the next. Among other things, it varies according to the physique of the individual.

The "years of drinking" are also relative. The time it takes a novice drinker to become an addict can be anywhere from one to twenty years.

The "euphoria level" is the point at which the drinker reaches Cloud Nine, forgets his inhibitions, and revels in his own fancied charm as well as that of others.

The "tolerance level" is the point at which he gets sick and can drink no more.

Both the alcoholic and non-alcoholic start their drinking histories with one thing in common it takes little alcohol to put them in high spirits and little more to make them sick.

As time passes, both require more alcohol to reach either level. But the alcoholic needs more and more. Because of the greater significance he gives to drinking, during pre-alcoholism years he may learn how to space his drinks and to some extent control his behavior. But he cannot manipulate his tolerance level. That is biologically determined.

There comes the time when the alcoholic's tolerance levels off. This is usually marked by a loss of control -- give him one drink and he is "off to the races." He has become addicted, physiologically dependent upon alcohol. From this point on, he continues to need more and more to escape everyday reality and regain a sense of euphoria. But his "capacity" before getting sick remains the same. As a result he can handle fewer and fewer drinks after he begins to feel carefree. But he cannot stop in that desirable state of bliss. He is compelled to keep drinking until he is physically unable to drink anymore.

Eventually there comes the day when he drinks just as much, but feels no sense of well-being at all. He only gets sick. (This is the point on the diagram where the tolerance and euphoria lines meet.) Desperately, he goes on benders in search of the alcoholic euphoria he is never to know again. He continues drinking, but gets sick sooner because his tolerance level is plunging down. He discovers that he cannot even keep up with the non-alcoholic friends whom he used to drink under the table any day in the week. One unproductive drink, maybe two, and he is through. His brain and the rest of the body have taken all the alcoholic abuse they can.

VII. PROGRESSIVE SYMPTOMS

The behavioral characteristics of the alcoholic are as progressive as his tolerance to alcohol and the course of the disease itself. They often enable the counselor to determine the relative status of a patient's addiction.

An inventory of some of those symptoms follows. They are not necessarily in precise chronological order. Some may never be experienced by an individual alcoholic. But most of them are experienced and, in toto, are mileposts along the way.

PRE-ADDICTION:

The road to alcoholism begins when drinking is no longer social but a means of psychological escape from the tensions and inhibitions. Although the eventual problem drinker is still in reasonable control, his habits begin to fall into a definite pattern:

1. Gross drinking behavior: He begins to drink more heavily and more often than his friends. "Getting tight" becomes a habit. When drunk, he may develop a "big shot" complex, recklessly spending money, boasting of real and fancied accomplishments, etc.

2. Blackouts: A "blackout," temporary loss of memory, is not to be confused with "pass-out,"

loss of consciousness. The drinker suffering from a blackout cannot remember things he said, things he did, places he visited while carousing the night before or for longer periods. Even a social drinker can have a blackout. With prospective alcoholics, they are more frequent and develop into a pattern.

3. <u>Gulping and sneaking drinks</u>: Anxious to maintain a euphoric level, he begins to toss off drinks at parties and slyly gulp down extra ones when he thinks nobody is looking. He may also "fortify himself" before going to a party to insure his euphoria. He feels guilty about this behavior and skittishly avoids talking about drinks or drinking.

4. <u>Chronic hangovers</u>: As he grows more and more reliant on alcohol as a shock absorber to daily living, "morning after" hangovers become more frequent and increasingly painful. (See "Physiological Effects," above.)

ADDICTION:

Until now the problem drinker has been imbibing heavily but not always conspicuously. More important, he has been able to stop drinking when he so chose. Beyond this point, he develops the symptoms of addiction with increased rapidity:

5. <u>Loss of control</u>: This is the most common symptom that a drinker's pschological habit has become an addiction. He still may refuse to accept a drink. But once he takes a drink, he cannot stop. A single drink is likely to trigger a chain reaction that will continue without a break into a state of complete intoxication.

6. <u>The alibi system</u>: His loss of control induces feelings of guilt and shame. So he concocts an elaborate system of "reasons" for drinking -- "he just completed his income tax," "he failed to complete his income tax," etc. He hopes these will justify his behavior in the eyes of his family and associates. In reality, they are mostly to reassure himself.

7. <u>Eye-openers</u>: He needs a drink in the morning "to start the day right." His morning" may start at any hour of day or night. So an eye-opener is in fact sedation to ease his jangled nerves, hangover, feelings of remorse, etc., after a period of involuntary abstinence, while he was asleep. He cannot face the upcoming hours without alcohol.

8. <u>Changing the pattern</u>: By now he is under pressure from his family, employer, or both. He tries to break the hold alcohol has on him. At first he may try changing brands -- e.g., from whiskey to beer. That docs not good. Then he may set up his own rules on when he will drink and what he will drink -- e.g., only three martinis on weekends and, of course, holidays. He may even "go on the wagon" for a period. Bat one sip of alcohol and the chain reaction starts all over again.

9. <u>Anti-social behavior</u>: He prefers drinking alone or only with other alcoholics, regardless of their social level. He believes that only they can understand him. He broods over imagined wrongs inflicted by others outside this pale and thinks people are staring at him or talking about him. He is highly critical of others and may become violent or destructive.

10. <u>Loss of friends and job</u>: His continuing anti-social behavior causes his friends to avoid him.

The aversion is now mutual. Members of his family may become so helplessly implicated that his wife leaves him "to bring him to his senses." The same situation develops between him, his employer and fellow" workers. And so he loses his job.

11. <u>Seeking medical aid</u>: Physical and mental erosion caused by uncontrolled drinking leads him to make the rounds of hospitals, doctors, psychiatrists, etc. But because he will not admit the extent of his drinking, he seldom receives any lasting benefit. Even when he does halfway "level" with the doctors, he fails to cooperate in following their instructions and the result is the same.

LAST STAGES:

Until he has reached this point, the alcoholic has had a choice: to drink or not to drink that first drink. Once he began, he lost all control. But in the last stages of alcoholism, he has no choice at all. He <u>must</u> drink:

12. <u>Benders</u>: He gets blindly and helplessly drunk for days at a time, hopelessly searching for that feeling of alcoholic euphoria he once appreciated. He utterly disregards everything -- family, job, food, even shelter. These periodic flights into oblivion might be called "drinking to escape the problems caused by drinking."

13. <u>Tremors</u>: In the past his hands may have trembled a bit on "mornings after." But now he gets "the shakes" when he is forced to abstain, a serious nervous condition which racks his whole body. When combined with hallucinations, they are known as the D.T.'s (delerium tremens), often fatal if medical help is not close at hand. During and immediately after an attack, he will swear off liquor forever. He nevertheless comes back for more of the same.

14. <u>Protecting the supply</u>: Having an immediate supply of alcohol available becomes the most important thing in his life to avoid the shakes, if nothing else. He will spend his last cent and, if necessary, sell the coat off his back to get it. Then he hides his bottles so there will always be a drink close at hand when he needs it which can be any hour or minute of day or night.

15. <u>Unreasonable resentments</u>: He shows hostility to others. This can be a conscious effort to protect his precious liquor supply, be it a half-pint on the hip or a dozen quarts secreted about the home. It can also be outward evidence of an unconscious desire to punish himself.

16. <u>Nameless fears and anxieties</u>: He becomes constantly fearful of things he cannot pin down nor describe in words. It is a feeling of impending doom or destruction. This adds to his nervousness and further underscores the compulsion to drink. These fears frequently crop up in the form of hallucinations, both auditory and visual.

17. <u>Collapse of the alibi system</u>: He finally realizes that he can no longer make excuses nor put the blame on others. He has to admit that the fanciful "reasons" he has been fabricating to justify his drinking are preposterous to others and now ridiculous to himself. This may have occurred to him several times during the course of his alcoholic career. But this time it is final. He has to admit that he is licked; that his drinking is beyond his ability to control.

18. <u>Surrender process</u>:   Now if ever, he must give up the idea of ever drinking again and be willing to seek and accept help.

If at this point the alcoholic is unable to surrender, all the signposts point to custodial care or death.

If he has not already suffered extensive and irreversible brain damage, there is a strong likelihood that some form of alcoholic psychosis will develop.

The amnesia and confabulation of Korsakoff's syndrome and the convulsions and comas of Wernicke's disease are possibilities.

Death may come in advanced cases of cirrhosis of the liver, pancreatitis, or hemorrhaging varices of the esophagus.

Or he may arrange his own death by suicide. After all, the suicide rate among alcoholics is three times the normal rate of self-extermination.

VIII. TREATMENT

There is as yet no cure for alcoholism.

The alcoholic is fortunate that the disease is treatable, that it can be arrested. But treatment is of no avail unless that addicted patient subscribes to total abstinence from drinking alcohol in any form. As pointed out above, once he has lost control, he will never regain it.

Also, the sooner the progress of the illness is recognized and arrested, the easier the return to a comfortable and contining sobriety and the less physical and mental deterioration.

The treatment of alcoholism falls into three overlapping lines of action designed for three overlapping objectives:

1. Emergency treatment: Immediate medication, etc., designed to avert physical
disaster or even death.

2. Inpatient treatment: "Drying out." To alleviate the nervous and physical
abnormalities resulting from prolonged and excessive drinking.

3. Follow-up treatment: Psychological rehabilitation necessary for continued sobriety.

Much of the data in the next two sections is for the alcoholism counselor's information only. The prescription and administration of medication and therapeutic procedures are the sole responsibility of authorized medical personnel. However, the counselor should be aware of general practices in order to help the patient and his family arrive at decisions.

A. EMERGENCY TREATMENT

Both acute alcoholic intoxication and many of the withdrawal symptoms which follow can call for prompt treatment in the emergency room of a general hospital.

However, before making a diagnosis of alcohol intoxication, the staff must rule out skull fracture, subdural or subarachnoid hemorrhage, cardio-vascular injury, and diabetic or insulin shock. These are quickly ascertained by laboratory and X-ray tests. Even though blood tests may indicate a high concentration of alcohol in the bloodstream, they do not veto the possibility that other factors may be the primary cause of his condition.

Once alcohol intoxication is diagnosed, it must be remembered that alcohol is in itself a powerful sedative. If the patient is in a stupor or in a comatose state, he should not be given any further sedation.

In cases where treatment for psychomotor agitation (e.g., "the shakes") is indicated, a tranquilizing drug such as Librium is highly effective in reducing tension. Many doctors feel that 100 mgs. given intramuscularly, then followed by smaller amounts taken orally every three or four hours for twelve to twenty-four hours, allow the body to adjust to the abrupt withdrawal of alcohol. Other tran-quilizers such as Thorazine, Sparine, Mellaril, Vistaril, Atarax, etc. are equally effective. An old standby, paraldehyde, has been largely eclipsed by newer drugs because of its habituating properties. Narcotics and barbituates should definitely be avoided because of even more habituating properties. They can only add further addictions to the addiction which already exists.

More serious and sometimes fatal are alcoholic coma, convulsions, hallucinosis and delirium tremens.

Before making a diagnosis of alcoholic coma, the following conditions must be ruled out: skull fracture, subdural or subarachnoid hemorrhage (bleeding in the membranes surrounding the brain), cardio-vascular accident (heart attack), uremia, insulin shock and diabetic coma.

One of the main dangers in alcoholic coma is a respiratory failure, followed by circulatory collapse. It may be necessary to maintain adequate airway to the lungs, use artificial respiration, and/or administer stimulants to the central nervous system. Another danger is the inhalation of vomited matter, which can cause lung abscess or pneumonia. Possible fractures and lacerations resulting from falls must also be considered.

Alcoholic convulsions ("rum fits") closely resemble the grand mal seizures of epilepsy. The examining physician should make certain by electroencephalogram (EEG) if necessary -- that the patient is not suffering from the latter disorder. The primary concern is that he does not injure himself in falling or thrashing about, or by biting or swallowing his tongue, which can cause him to choke to death. A spoon, a leather belt or any device he cannot bite through should be inserted between his teeth. Valium is a useful drug in controlling the attack. To prevent such attacks, Dilantin, an anticonvulsant, is prescribed for alcoholics with a history of seizures.

Alcoholic hallucinosis usually occurs after a patient has been detoxified The hallucinations can be either auditory or visual, with the former more common. They are not as frightening as the fantastic figments encountered during D.T.'s and the patient is usually oriented as to time, place and the existing situation. There is danger of suicide and the patient should be watched.

Delirium tremens (D.T.'s) is a withdrawal symptom which can occur many days after the alcoholic has stopped drinking and, when not immediately treated, can be fatal. As the name implies, it combines visual and auditory hallucinations with extreme tremors and even grand mal type convulsions. Unlike alcoholic hallucinosis, the patient is completely disoriented. His hallucinations take the form of grotesque human and animal ghouls which threaten him from every side. He should be treated in a well lighted room because every shadow can conjure up another evil menace to panic him. An attending nurse, counselor or other aide should not argue about the existence of these phantasms -- only reassure the patient that nobody will harm him. Librium, Vistaril, chlorpromazines and other tranquilizers are used in treatment.

(The gravity of D.T.'s cannot be overemphasied. In a situation where a patient shows signs of impending D.T.'s and no medical help is available, he can be given an ounce or two of whiskey or fortified wine. This will help to stave off the attack until he can be handed over to a hospital emergency room.)

Coma, convulsions, hallucinosis and D.T.'s are definite medical emergencies and should be treated in the hospital until the patient has fully recovered from the immediate crisis.

In other cases of acute phases of chronic alcoholism, if the patient is not too ill he may be discharged in the care of a cooperative family or interested person who will follow medical instructions.

In any event, the patient must be directed to follow up his emergency room treatment by seeing his family doctor, coming back to the hospital's outpatient clinic, or arranging for continued treatment at a public or private alcoholism clinic. This is for his own protection as well as that of the hospital and personnel who attended him.

B. IMPATIENT TREATMENT

Then there are the hundreds, even thousands of non-emergency patients whose prolonged and excessive drinking has left them so mentally and physically "run down" that they are incapable of adequately dealing with their responsibilities at home or on the job. Simply to let them sleep off their drunks or give them tranquilizers to cushion their shakes and then send them on their ways is inviting trouble. Most of then will wander into the nearest tavern or liquor store and promptly find themselves in worse trouble than they were before -- back again in "the revolving door."

What they need is "drying out," both physical and mental. They need to start repairing the damage the persistent drinking has done to their bodies. They need to disentangle their confused thinking before they can even grasp the meaning of any new program of rehabilitation.

For these persons the best solution is six to eight days hospitalization. In this way, constant care and medication is assured. If they suffer withdrawal symptoms -- such as hallucinosis or D.T's -- there is professional help at hand for immediate treatment, or even to avert the attacks. Above all, they are removed from the temptation of sneaking drinks that often undo the good of treatment at home.

Patients are usually kept on bed rest for the first twenty-four hours after admission, during which they are given routine laboratory and X-ray tests. There will be psychomotor agitation as the patient's body adjusts to the abrupt withdrawal of alcohol. Tranquilizers such as Librium, Sparine, Mellaril, Thorazine, Vistaril, or Atarax will keep him in a state of quiet suspense for the first 36 to 48 hours and are gradually tapered off as his condition improves.

At the same time steps are taken to correct the vitamin-mineral deficiency which has been building up over the days, weeks, or months the patient has been drinking instead of eating. He is put on a high protein diet and multivitamins. Orange juice, with a dash of sodium chloride in it, is kept at his bedside. And in cases of severe dehydration, he is given "Philadelphia cocktails" intravenously, which contain a glucose-saline solution, insuline, and vitamins.

As this period of rest and recuperation progresses, his thinking begins to straighten out. This is the time to lay the groundwork for follow-up treatment. He must be made to realize that recovery from chronic alcoholism is not an overnight or eight-day procedure. The damage has been years in the making. Even with his sincere cooperation, it takes one or two years to make basic psychological and physical repairs. This is the time to line him up for continuing treatment at an outpatient clinic, Alcoholics Anonymous, or other therapeutic agencies.

During this period, the patient may also be started on Antabuse (see "Deterrent Therapy," below).

C. FOLLOW-UP TREATMENT

The chronic alcoholic cannot stay sober without help. (One hears of the person who "did it on his own," but one seldom meets him in the flesh.)

The alcoholic needs support. He should have the encouragement of family and friends, if he has any left. But the support of family and friends can be erratic and is not to be found in some areas where he needs help the most.

He constantly needs to remember that he is an alcoholic who cannot afford to take a drink without unfortunate results just as the diabetic cannot afford to forget his ailment and his insulin, or the epileptic his Dilantin.

For years the alcoholic has been committing physical and mental hara-kiri and he may need prolonged medical or psychiatric help.

Alcoholism can be expensive; and, therefore, the patient may be broke. Alcoholism loses jobs; he may need employment. Alcoholism causes dissension; he may seek reconciliation with his family. And so on.

Unless he is spiritually barren, he can be kept reminded of his vulnerability in Alcoholics Anonymous, as well as find understanding and moral support (see below). But if he is in need of professional help and advice in addition to awareness and understanding, an alcoholism clinic is probably his one best resource.

The many roles played by outpatient clinics are described in the next chapter. In brief, their primary concerns are medical and psychiatric services, and individual and group counseling. These are geared to meet the needs of alcoholics at large as well as hospital dischargees.

The medical and psychiatric services can range from consultation and referrals to critical treatment-on-the-spot, depending upon facilities.

The medical and psychiatric services can range from consultation and referrals to critical treatment-on-the-spot, depending upon facilities.

Individual counseling is available to help the patient work out solutions to his very personal problems. This service is hot intended to act as an employment or public welfare resource. But the counselor should be able to refer the patient to appropriate agencies in the community to meet these and other special needs.

Group counseling or "group therapy," to use the term in its broad non-professional sense is the outpatient clinic's major contribution to continued treatment once a patient has emerged from the mental and physical distress of intoxication, and withdrawal.

Continued sobriety can only be achieved by changing the alcoholic's attitude and teaching him new ways of dealing with the frustrations that drove him to drink.

In this type of treatment, the patient is assigned to a small, ongoing group of fellow alcoholics who discuss their common "hang-ups" -- i.e., frustrations and temptations which led to their past drinking -- and what they are doing to meet them without resorting to alcohol. A trained leader -- usually a psychiatrist, psychiatric nurse, social worker or counselor -- merely keeps the discussion within bounds. At first, the new patient is inclined to confine his participation and mental note-taking to alcohol, its use and misuse. As he becomes better acquainted with the other members of the group, he finds himself more and more involved in the discussion of more stressful areas of personal and social functioning. Accordingly, the way is cleared for greater insight into his own personality and behavior and those elements which have contributed to his alcoholism. He is then better able to adapt himself to a more meaningful way of living without recourse to alcohol.

Many psychiatrists feel that group therapy is far more effective than individual psychotherapy. Because of the alcoholic's habit of "sneaking" drinks, protecting his supply, and feelings of guilt, he becomes more and more of a "loner" as his illness progresses. In group treatment he once again becomes physically and psychologically involved with other people. Thus, he is pried loose from the isolation, he has built up for himself not by choice, but because his disease demanded it.

(Both individual and group counseling are more fully discussed in Chapter III.)

D. DETERRENT THERAPY

Disulfiram (Antabuse) is a drug often prescribed to deter the alcoholic from drinking. It is no "cure." It does not erase the desire to drink. But it does make the consequences of drinking the slightest amount of alcohol so agonizing that even the most confirmed dipsomaniac will abstain so long as it remains in his system.

Normally the liver oxidizes alcohol into acetaldehyde which, in turn, breaks down into acetic acid and next into carbon dioxide and water. Acetaldehyde is a poison. Necessary for its breakdown is a enzyme (acetaldehyde dehydrogenase) which the disulfiram blocks. When this happens, the acetaldehyde rapidly accumulates and within a few minutes, the patient becomes violently ill. He becomes extremely hot and flushed. His blood pressure rises rapidly and a splitting headache develops. Concurrently, he develops a pain in the chest which spreads into the left arm, his heart pounds rapidly, and he finds it difficult to breathe. Suddenly, his blood pressure falls and. he may become sick to the stomach and even collapse. He then falls into a deep sleep.

The attack may last up to four hours; but the patient shudders at the thought of experiencing it again.

However, Antabuse has no effect upon the body unless alcohol is taken. It needs a detonator to start the chain reaction. And the only detonator is a drink.

Thus, it acts as or silent policeman to protect the patient's abstinence. The average practicing alcoholic cannot envision life without his favorite beverage to sustain him. Once he starts on an Antabuse regimen, he discovers that sobriety is not only attainable and endurable, but that it can be more agreeable than the way things were with alcohol.

By itself, Antabuse is no panacea to bring about and maintain sobriety. But taken regularly, it acts as a shield against impulsive "slips" which can be serious setbacks in continuing treatment. Once the patient takes his daily dose, he has no decisions to make about drinking or not drinking for the next 72 hours. And it keeps him sober to profit from whatever form of follow-up therapy he may be undergoing.

On the other hand, if a patient who claims that he is "on Antabuse" drinks with no ill effects, the therapist knows that he is not taking his medication as prescribed. It can be reasonably assumed that he has not yet achieved the motivation necessary for any program of recovery.

Because of the reactions that occur when alcohol is taken on top of Antabuse, the patient must have a physical examination before the drug can be prescribed. (Contraindications include uncontrolled hypertension (high blood pressure), coronary heart disease, late stages of cirrhosis, severe pancreatitis, psychoses or brain damage, and sometimes pregnancy.) The patient is given a card to carry with him so he will not be given medication containing alcohol in the event of an emergency. Antabuse should not be administered until 72 hours have elapsed since the patient's last drink; nor should he drink again until at least 72 hours after taking his last pill.

E. MISCELLANEOUS THERAPIES

There are many other types of therapy, most of which the alcoholism counselor will probably never hear about. But there arc several of which he should be aware:

Lysergic acid (LSD) therapy: Research continues on this still unproved method of treatment. Thus far the effectiveness apparently rests in the degree of rapport established between the patient and the individual therapist who attends him on his "trips."

Hypnosis: Used in certain types of psychiatric and psychosomatic illnesses, some practitioners believe hypnosis can be employed in the treatment of alcoholism. Up to now the results have not been very successful.

Conditioned response therapy: The most common of many procedures is to add an emetic to a patient's favorite brand of alcoholic beverage. After several nauseating experiences, he is automatically supposed to develop a distast for the stuff. Chief drawbacks are: (1) that frequent "reconditioning" is necessary; and (2) that patients can often switch to other brands and continue drinking without ill effects.

<u>Psychodrama</u>: This is a form of group therapy wherein the patients act out psychic conflicts. Because of the highly emotional nature of these conflicts, psychodrama should only be employed under the close supervision of a psychiatrist or specially trained psychodrama therapist.

F. ALCOHOLICS ANONYMOUS

Alcoholics Anonymous is a fellowship of problem drinkers who have banded together in an effort to help themselves and other problem drinkers attain sobriety.

Their program is best summed up in "Twelve Steps" which the members are urged to follow:

1. We admitted we were powerless over alcohol -- that our lives had become unmanageable.
2. Cane to believe that a Power greater than ourselves could restore us to sanity.
3. Made a decision to turn our will and our lives over to the care of God as we understood Him.
4. Made a searching and fearless moral inventory of ourselves.
5. Admitted to God, to ourselves, and to another human being the exact nature of our wrongs.
6. Were entirely ready to have God remove all these defects of character.
7. Humbly asked Him to remove our shortcomings.
8. Made a list of all persons we had harmed, and became willing to make amends to them all.
9. Made direct amends to such people wherever possible, except when to do so would injure them or others.
10. Continued to take personal inventory and when we were wrong promptly admitted it.
11. Sought through prayer and meditation to improve our conscious contact with God as we understood Him, praying only for knowledge of His will for us and the power to carry that out.
12. Having had a spiritual awakening as the result of these steps, we tried to carry this message to alcoholics, and to practice these principles in all our affairs.

While "God" is frequently mentioned in these steps, A.A. members are quick to point out that they "adhere to no particular creed or religion" and welcome agnostics into the fellowship. But the spiritual element does play an important role in the "therapy."

Undoubtedly, A.A. has been responsible for many recoveries in the United States and in other countries. This is not surprising in view of its half million members including those not affiliated with any one group and the profusion of those groups, which are to be found in practically any sizable community in the country. With "no dues or fees in A.A.," with no rosters kept (to insure anonymity), with no record of those who may attend one or two meetings and then disappear from sight, it is impossible to estimate the percentage of recoveries. But by the sheer weight of the number of alcoholics exposed, any head-count would be high.

A.A. meetings are either "open" or "closed." Anyone interested in the program, alcoholic or non-alcoholic, can attend the former. Closed meetings are for alcoholics only. They are usually sessions in which the participants discuss more intimate alcoholic experiences. Both meetings are presided over by members chosen on a rotating, week-to-week basis -- i.e., no special training is involved.

One consideration in a sick alcoholic's limiting his treatment to A.A. is the fact that there is no medical or psychiatric screening. A "Twelfth Step worker" enthused over his own improvement, may be apt to disregard an underlying mental or physical disorder that is contributing to the woes of the person who has called for help. But on the whole, A.A.'ers are becoming increasingly aware of the physiological and psychiatric complications of the disease. More realize that "first things come first" and that physical and mental blocks must be overcome before the ailing alcoholic is ready to comprehend the spiritual.

Many clinic patients regularly attend A.A. meetings, just as many A.A. members find additional support in clinical therapy and Antabuse.

All reliable resources must be used in treating the alcoholic. So the alcoholism counselor should keep schedules of area A.A. meetings on hand at all times. Alcoholics Anonymous has proved its worth.

COUNSELING THE ALCOHOLIC

CONTENTS

I. PHILOSOPHY AND PRINCIPLES	1
II. THREE STAGES OF RELATIONSHIP	1
III. THE INITIAL INTERVIEW	2
IV. THE CONTINUING RELATIONSHIP	4
V. GROUP COUNSELING	5
VI. GROUP THERAPY AND A. A.	7

COUNSELING THE ALCOHOLIC

I. PHILOSOPHY AND PRINCIPLES

The alcoholic who is not ready to undergo treatment will often protest,. "Only an alcoholic can help an alcoholic!"

That is not true.

But the counselor -- alcoholic or non-alcoholic --who would help the man or woman whose life is disintegrating because of drinking should thoroughly understand the physical and emotional pain involved before attempting to establish rapport.

The essential quality is one of empathy, which the dictionary defines as "the capacity for participating in another's feelings or ideas." It differs from sympathy in that the counselor does not become emotionally involved, allowing the patient's joys and sorrows to affect his own ability to evaluate and advise.

The effective counselor must not only be able to understand others. He must have a real desire to understand others, to explore the whys of human behavior. And he must have an unconditional, positive regard for the individual patient -- a blend of warmth, acceptance, regard, interest, and respect.

He must continually work on his own self-awareness. He should recognize his own hang-ups and learn to deal with them. One who is able to do this is better able to be a partner in a helping relationship.

He must always remember that he is a counselor, not an analyst nor a judge. Overconcern with personality theories and counseling techniques will endanger rapport, just as premature attempts to arrive at solutions will surely lead to the patient's being short-changed.

Equipped with a knowledge of the physiological and psychological nature of alcoholism and especially of its progressive symptoms, the trained counselor usually is in a position to assess the general status of the new patient who sits before him. He has a broad idea of the physical pains, emotional distress, and changing attitudes the alcoholic has already suffered. This may be a small start. But it is an important head start in winning acceptance and evolving a program for recovery.

From that point on it is the counselor's job to translate his general observations into full and meaningful particulars about the highly individual person who seeks his help. Once that is accomplished, they can work together towards reasonable decisions and practical steps to be taken.

II. THREE STAGES OF RELATIONSHIP

Effective relationships between alcoholism counselors and their patients can be broken down into three stages:

The _first_ might be called the subjective period. During this, usually the initial interview, the counselor wins the patient's confidence and establishes his empathy with him. He then gathers as much pertinent information as possible -- e.g., personal data, marriage and family status, employment, hospitalizations and arrests, drinking habits, etc.

The _second_ is an objective stage. The counselor points out to the pa-tient his current status in comparison with known patterns and established facts about the disease. He explains what could lie ahead.

The _third_ stage is one of teamwork. The counselor joins with the patient in building a road to recovery and solving the problems still posed by the past.

III. THE INITIAL INTERVIEW

   A. <u>Importance</u>

The initial interview usually is the most important, not only because "first impressions" tend to linger on, but because it may also be the last.

For a variety of reasons, the counselor may never again set eyes upon his patient. One of the most common -- particularly in outpatient clinics -- is that the patient is not sufficiently motivated to undergo continuing treatment. At the moment, the prospect of a lifetime without drinking is too frightening. He should nevertheless leave the counselor's office knowing that the door will always be open to him, tomorrow or ten years hence.

A sense of security is the key to gaining the new patient's confidence so that he will come back.

So the patient must be satisfied that the counselor will respect whatever confidences he may choose to divulge. He must be reasonably confident that the counselor is not going to berate him as he has been berated in the past. He must be assured that he can lower his defenses and receive understanding instead of recrimination.

The counselor cannot expect to be told pertinent confidences unless the patient has confidence in him.

   B. <u>The Contract</u>
Also in the initial interview, a "contract" should be established.

The patient must be aware that alcoholism is an illness -- not a sin or a sign of weakness of character. Whether or not he is suffering from that illness will be up to him to decide, if he has not already done so.

If the answer is yes, he has two choices: to accept treatment or to continue drinking. If he chooses the latter, probably, eventually, it will result in custodial care or death.

However, if he sincerely wants to recover, he must accept the fact that he is a sick man who can no longer drink. The counselor and his colleagues cannot do this for him. But they can help him help himself.

Such are the essentials of the initial contract. The counselor can make them clear in any way that best befits the situation or the patient's general attitude at the time. But unless the patient subscribes to them, any recovery program is courting failure.

C. Eliciting Patient History

The primary concern in a counselor-patient relationship is "Where do we go from here?" But significant facts about the patient's past and present are necessary for any reliable estimate of the situation.

In the course of time, counselors develop their individual methods of eliciting this information. So it would be presumptuous here to advance any hard-and-fast rules about interviewing new patients as one would instruct a student in the operation of a computer. However, there are certain basic principles to be considered.

The truism that "the quality of the answer depends upon the quality of the question" is universally accepted. The patient must be made to feel that he has the interviewer's undivided attention. He can perceive the presence or lack of empathy not only by the questions asked, but also by the counselor's overall manner. The tone of voice can be more persuasive than the questions themselves. Questions that reflect accusation and suspicion on the part of the counselor arouse resentment and suspicion in the patient and can quickly erase whatever rapport has been established in the beginning.

Even the pacing should be adjusted to the patient. Too slow a pace may suggest a difficulty in understanding on the part of the counselor. Too fast a pace can imply lack of interest.

Some questions must of necessity be pointed and direct e.g., date of birth, marital status, employment, etc. Those are to be expected. Other pointed questions - such as those dealing with the patient's parental and childhood background - are more readily answered if the purpose in asking them is explained. But,in general, pithy questions are preferable to those that can be answered yes or no. They can lead to greater insight into the patient's personality.

D. Problems and Solutions

Then there is the question that slams the door. The patient "clams up." More often than not it touches upon a painful memory which triggers the frigid reaction. It is useless to pursue the point at that time. The counselor can come back to it later in the interview or, as often happens, the patient will inadvertently supply the answer while responding to another evocative question.

In the same category are evasions and obvious lies. Few alcoholics will admit to having more than "a couple of beers" before their accidents, arrests,or other plights. The first meeting is no time to break down their defenses. Usually "the truth will out" -- that the patient had a pint and a half of whiskey between the two beers -- before the interview is over. The counselor should accept both the lie and its disproval without comment. The same holds true for other camouflages thrown up by the patient.

Nor are all answers verbal. The counselor should listen to what the patient does not say, as well as to what he says. The omissions in his explanations and comments are frequently more revealing than the explanations themselves. At the same time, physical clues can also be expressive of the emotional attitude -- e.g., the sweaty palms arising from fear or a sense of guilt, the folded arms of contrariness, the tears of sheer frustration and self-pity.

The most empathic alcoholism counselor in the world could not hope for a perfect batting average among all the applicants who come to him for aid. Perfect rapport cannot be arranged by an admission desk. Sometimes a patient might better be counseled by a worker in the next room or one down the hall. Or he may gravitate to a new group leader, even after weeks of individual counseling by the person who first interviewed him. In such cases, the counselor should have no hesitancy in "letting the patient go."

E. Problems that the Counselor Cannot Solve

The counselor must be able to distinguish between the patients he can help and those he cannot. He should recognize his own capabilities and limitations. It may be that a difficult family or financial situation or some other involved personal problem is causing or substantially contributing to the patient's drinking. When it is apparent that the cause, whatever it may be, is beyond the counselor's ability to help, he should refer the patient to an agency which can.

IV. THE CONTINUING RELATIONSHIP

Most of the above observations also apply to the continuing counselor-patient relationship. Of course, once the ice has been broken in the initial interviews and confidence established, the alcoholic is not apt to revert to lies and evasions with his counselor or physician. If he has normal intelligence, he will have found out that frankness best paves the way for significant planning and decisions.

Nor are there any precise ground rules to guide the counselor in an ongoing relationship. Success lies in adapting himself to the patient's attitude and, through empathy, helping him to plan ways and means of reaching the goals he sincerely wants to reach. In other words, the counselor has to "play it by ear."

A. Basics

But there are several basic "rules of thumb."

In planning ways and means of reaching objectives, final decisions should be made by the patient, not by the counselor.

One must remember that the average alcoholic comes glutted with unasked-for advice -- opinionated guidance supplied by family, parents, employer, best friend, and well-meaning companions. The patient is tired of advice.

So even if the counselor should know the answers, he should forego the role of mastermind. Better he discuss the pros and cons until the patient can view himself and his situation in the cold light of reality and decide for himself what had best be done to remedy matters. This is not to say that the counselor cannot offer alternatives, nor should he allow the patient to decide upon a potentially disastrous course of action. But when the patient himself makes the final decision or believes that he made it -- it becomes a strictly personal matter. It is no longer advice from family, parents, employer, or best friend. It is his own decision and, as such, he has greater confidence in the chances for success, especially with the counselor and his resources to lend support.

B. Constructive Forces

Besides being surfeited with advice, the average alcoholic comes oppressed with feelings of guilt and inferiority and loss of self-respect. The counselor should search out the constructive forces in his client. He must believe in them and their potentialities. And then he must make the patient realize them and believe in them, too. He can always cite the truism that every man is superior to the next man in some respect -- physically, psychologically, or intellectually. Once that asset is recognized, it can become another steppingstone in planning the road to recovery.

One of the beneficial by-products of counseling is catharsis the process by which repressed emotions and memories are brought to consciousness and released. It is an outpouring of emotionally painful thoughts which the patient has been harboring inside himself with perhaps no one available to console or consult, and which he has futile-ly been attempting to drown in drink. The counselor-patient relationship offers an opportunity for such purgative relief.

Catharsis should be fostered, but not forced. As he listens, the counselor should be alert to responses by the patient which reflect feeling rather than mere recollection, emotions rather than intellect. Strongly felt sentiments can reveal themselves at almost any time e.g., while talking about the family's reaction to his drinking, difficulties on the job, strained relation in the community. The bald recital of an occurrence may impulsively be punctuated with the patient's emotional reaction to the event. This is the time for the counselor to encourage him to express his feelings instead of just facts. But his questions and comments should be leading rather than probing, persuasive rather than pressing. Otherwise the patient may crawl back into his private world and slam the door behind him.

V. GROUP COUNSELING

As a general rule alcoholics are more effectively treated in group therapy than in the traditional one-to-one counselor-patient relationship.

This does not mean that the patient's need for individual counseling is completely superseded when he becomes a member of a group. Strictly personal problems may arise. Help from outside resources may be needed. Periods of uncertainty and depression may threaten his new self-command. In such cases, he may need individual counseling for support.

But for ongoing therapy the group affords a climate which the alcoholic has been avoiding for months or even years. Hiding his drinking habits from others or protecting his supply, he has usually become a loner. As participant in a group, he again becomes a member of society a society in miniature, perhaps, but nevertheless, a cooperative body with common aims and interests. It evokes intercommunication and, hopefully, interaction with others so necessary in again facing up to reality and normal living.

This escape from isolation is only one of many benefits a patient can derive from group therapy. The interpersonal relationships with others faced with the same illness gradually reduces his own sensitivity. He finds understanding, reassurance, and support. As time goes on, he gains greater insight into the origins and evolution of his behavior patterns. He is re-educated in ways of adapting himself to reality. And, because the environment is real, not artificial, he can test many of those ways within the group itself.

A. Role of the Group Leader

The group leader -- be he alcoholism counselor, social worker, or psychiatrist -- must always remember that the group belongs to its members. His primary mission is to be a good listener, with any outward participation kept to a minimum. The members must feel that they are the ones who are choosing the questions for discussion, arriving at the answers, settling any conflicts or confrontations.

However passive his role may appear to be, the leader must see to it that the discussion does not wander too far away from the subject. He should encourage participation by the silent minority, if any. He should act to relieve tensions and mediate debates. And, at all times, he should be noting the actions and reactions of the individual members, for these are clues to their progress in the recovery program.

While all these duties might seem to conflict with the leader's role as passive observer, he can usually delegate action to others.

Every group is made up of as many different personalities as there are members. They unconsciouly tend to assume various roles which they continue to play week after week. The leader can usually count upon them to function as needed. Among them are: The

Initiator -- introduces new ideas or subjects for discussion.
Information-seeker -- asks for pertinent facts.
Information-giver, -- always ready to supply those pertinent facts if he can.
Elaborator -- develops others' comments and ideas.
Orienter -- raises questions about the direction of discussion.
Coordinator -- tries to pull ideas and suggestions together.
Tester -- checks whether the group is ready for decision.
Opinion-giver -- states what he believes to be the consensus of the group.
Such members -- and other members in other roles -- are the group leader's advocates.

B. Measuring the Success of the Group

Superficially, it might seem easiest to measure the success of any group by the faithful attendance of its members and its attraction of new members.

But the true effectiveness of a group is best reflected in its contribution to its members' recovery. From time to time, the leader should ask himself these questions:

Has our group created an atmosphere in which constructive progress can be made?

Has it achieved real communication among members?

Do the members freely give and freely receive help?

Are the conditions such that each member can make his own special contribution?

Does it allow conflict and confrontation to be resolved into creative problem solving?

Has it evolved acceptable ways of making decisions?

If the leader can answer yes to all of these questions, he and the group are accomplishing their mission. If not, he had better diagnose the shortcomings and repair them.

VI. GROUP THERAPY AND A.A.

One frequently hears Alcoholics Anonymous vaguely referred to as "group psychotherapy."

In reality, there are many basic differences between the two methods of treatment. But a layman's misunderstanding can be forgiven since both have one aim among others -- to help the alcoholic stop drinking.

The counselor should be aware of these differences because the confusion is a common one.

A. <u>Differences Between the Two Methods</u>

In balancing method, it is best to disregard A.A.'s open meetings, where the general public is invited to attend, and limit comparisons to A.A.'s closed meetings, for alcoholics only.

Both A.A. and clinical groups are open to all alcoholics regardless of race, sex, or socio-economic status. While the latter are deliberately kept heterogeneous, members of A.A. tend to gravitate to groups composed of racial and socio-economic peers.

Both stress confidentiality. Outside visitors are not allowed. A.A. closed meetings do not permit the non-alcoholic spouses of members to attend. Clinical groups, recognizing alcoholism as a family disease, urge participation by members' families.

So long as alcoholic patients are under clinical treatment, they are required to attend group meetings, which are usually limited in size -- preferably six to nine participants. A.A. members are not required to attend meetings. Nor are there any limitations as to size. Hence, the same group can vary greatly from week to week in both numbers and make-up.

Leadership in clinical groups is vested in a trained psychotherapist or alcoholism counselor who unobtrusively steers discussion, mediates differences, and, when called upon, answers pertinent questions concerning alcohol and alcoholism. A.A. groups are presided over by a chairman, usually selected weekly on a rotating basis. The only requirement is to be an abstaining alcoholic.

The cornerstone of A.A. therapy is belief in a "God as one understands Him" and reliance upon His power to effect "a spiritual awakening" which will support a new, continuing life without alcohol. Catharsis and reparation for past wrongs committed against others are intended to alleviate guilt. Identification with other members who have succeeded in the program is stressed. Abstinence is the goal.

Clinical therapy, on the other hand, centers on psychological aspects. The alcoholic's nonrational and fantastic life theme is brought out and, through inter-communication and interaction with other group members, is eventually accepted by the patient and hopefully altered. The strengthening of relationships with other group members develops a sense of responsibility both for himself and for others. Full sobriety, not merely abstinence, is the goal.

In A.A., life membership is encouraged for continuing support. In clinical therapy, the successful member eventually leaves the group and stands on his own.

There are other differences, but these are the basic ones. The two therapies do not contravene one another. For many patients, they complement each other. When such is the case, the alcoholic can profitably embrace both.

www.ingramcontent.com/pod-product-compliance
Lightning Source LLC
Chambersburg PA
CBHW081817300426
44116CB00014B/2399